ACKNOWLEDGEMENTS

To all the coaches and basketball wizards who
instructed and inspired me along the way.

Mike "Wally" Martin

Tim Collins

Jeff Moore

Terry Buckner

Dwight Martin

Don Meyer

Bob Hurley

Jason Shelton

Dick Devenzio

David Snow

Kevin Griffin

Mike Erhart

Terry Evans

DeWayne "Lefty" Glascock

Ross Boucher

Scott Oatsvall

Rick Johnson

Anthony "EZ" Easter

Jody Bailey

Mike Chitty

Dan Wadley

Bobby White

Randy Scallions

Chris Randall

Larry Skinner

Frankie Willingham

Brent Windom

And Kevin Templeton

To all of my teammates who added so much joy to the game, competed like wild animals, but loved like human beings. It was an honor my friends.

COLLEGE

Ryan Alexander

Scott Weldy

Steve Robison

Scotty Collier

Zach Martin

Drew Murphy

Aaron Young

Rob Moore

Quincy Young

Scott McDonald

Chandler King

Craig Price

Brad Green

Keith Galloway

Andre Dubois

Nathan "Big Game" Ranew

Travis Williams

Travis Jackson

Mirek Holan

Blake Kirby

Caleb Marcum

David "V" Casteel

Phil Cudd

Joe McDowell

Jesse Baker

John Maples

Toree Ingram

Bob Richey

Javier Sanchez

Adam Asberry

Josh Jones

Daniel Jones

Danny Lancaster

Adam Mott

Todd Cahill

Higgs

HIGH SCHOOL

Nathan Templeton

Joey Cash

Danny Deas

Jeremy Kennedy

Anthony Johnson

Aaron McGuirt

Matt Neal

Brent Mink

David Burkhart

Gabe Johnson

Ricky Gossett

Braucht Walters

Matt Moore

Phil Cudd

Caleb Marcum

David "V" Casteel

Higgs- My only 9-year teammate

Joel Money

Eric Kee

Jeff Carter

Daniel Moore

David "Sweet T" Tiffin

Lance Walters

Jeron Williams

Johnny Hutchison

THANK YOU!

I Played for My

Dad for 9 Years,

AND WE
STILL TALK.

By Josh Templeton

I Played For My Dad For 9 Years, And We Still Talk

First Printing, 2016

Designed by Ryan Anderson

Edited by Coleman Rose and Lori Hawkins

Photo Credits: pp. 11, 18, 38, 39, 54, 62, 69, 111, 141, 153, 179, 181, 182, 185, 194, 211, 228, 231, and 240 photos are from the author's collection; pp. 34, 43, 104, 135, 158, 161, and 163 used by permission of The Chattanooga Times Free Press; pp. 157, 160, 162, and 169 photos by Stephen Kellogg

ISBN 978-0-9980624-0-2

A.I. Books 8436 Standifer Gap Rd. Chattanooga, TN 37421

This book is dedicated to my beautiful, loving wife Abbie, whose encouragement and friendship inspires me to be the best version of myself.

And to my father Kevin Templeton, who taught me how to be a man and let me be my own.

And to my brother Mitch, loved by all, stranger to none.

I Played for My
Dad for 9 Years,

And We
Still Talk.

PROLOGUE

THE LOCKER ROOM WAS quiet. The mood was serious. In less than 30 minutes we would be playing for a national championship. I sat on a bench between Caleb and Keith and started to pull out the contents of my bag. I pulled my trademark high red socks over my taped ankles, then laced up my Team Edition Nike Shox. I looked in my bag. Only one thing left. My white Temple #3 jersey. I held it in my hands. This would be the last time I put it on, and the last game I ever played.

As I sat there deep in thought, Dad walked in. Everyone was silent. He was a master in the art of pre-game motivation, and all eyes were locked on him as he began his speech.

"I want you to close your eyes."

"Think of the moments in your basketball journey that got you to this point. Sitting in this room. Getting ready to play for a national championship."

"I want you to remember why you started playing in the first place."

"See yourself as a little kid. A little kid playing the game for the sheer joy of playing."

"See yourself in the gym. Putting up shots with no one around."

"See yourself playing your best and celebrating the greatest moments of your career."

"Then visualize what you are about to do. See yourself playing the best game of your career in the national championship."

"See yourself cutting down the nets with your brothers."

"Don't move, just keep your eyes closed and take your journey."

A familiar piano tune began to play. Dave Barrett's *One Shining Moment* would be the soundtrack to our visualization journey. As the song played, I could see the moments just as if they were happening right then.

Battling on the outdoor courts of Highland Park...

Shirtless, soaked in sweat, putting up a shot in the dimly lit Vance Gym...

A bear hug from Higgs after winning the district championship...

The opening tip of the state championship game...

Breaking down in the locker room after the end of my high school career...

Draining a 3 and seeing Brad run the entire sideline taunting thousands of fans...

Dishing it off to Craig for a game sealing 3 pointer at Paul Dana Walker Arena...

Holding up the Region Championship banner with my boys...

As the final notes faded out, I could see myself cutting down the nets.

When I opened my eyes. Dad was standing in front of us.

"This is your moment. Go get it."

PART 1

THE FIRE

1

IT WAS A SNOWY Saturday in 1987 in Lima, Ohio. I was 7 years old and in that waking up early stage that I'm sure drove my parents crazy. I sat in my room playing G. I. Joes vs. He-Man. This was a time when kids still let their imaginations run wild and played with toys. It was so early it was still dark outside. Just as Skeletor was recruiting Snake Eyes to join him in his quest for world domination, Dad peeked into my room.

"I'm going to practice, Josh."

"Can I come?" I replied.

"Of course you can. Get your clothes on Big Dog."

I was pumped. I had never gone to practice with Dad on a Saturday before. Sure, I was always running around the gym after school when the guys were practicing. But I was usually playing hide and seek with a friend or getting into some random 7-year-old mischief. I was definitely not there for basketball, and Dad never asked me to be.

When we arrived at the gym, Dad brought out the basketballs and I grabbed one off the rack. I started dribbling like a maniac being dragged around wherever the ball took me, and occasionally throwing the ball toward the basket while he swept the floor with a dust mop.

"Lookin' good buddy," Dad said.

Meanwhile, the high school players started to file in one by one and lace up their Reebok Pumps. Jaden Callahan was the team's best player. He was 6'5" tall, played above the rim, and had a sweet stroke from behind the arc. To me, he was larger than life. Jaden didn't wear the Reebok Pumps. He wore the 1st edition Air Jordan sneaks, and I wanted to be just like him.

This time, for some reason, I didn't go off to my usual shenanigans when practice started. I came to practice with Dad on a Saturday, so I was into it. After showing off my unimpressive dribbling and shooting skills, I got some high fives from the guys.

Dad came up to me and gave me two options: "You can go run around and play, or you can be on the team as our manager for the day. Your job will be to get the guys water and towels when they need it. What'll it be, Big Dog?"

Without giving it a second thought I said, "Be on the team."

Dad smiled at me with this look, one that I'll never forget. A look that said, 'So you're ready to come along for the ride? We are gonna have so much fun.'

Oh man, I was beaming. I couldn't wait to show him I was a good helper. The idea of being a part of the team made me feel like a big boy, even if only for this one day.

I watched in awe as the guys did drill after drill and raced up and down the floor for 2 hours. When a player completed a rep and approached the sideline dripping with sweat, I would be there waiting with a towel and water bottle in my hands. During one of the competitive drills, Jaden threw down a vicious two handed dunk and approached the baseline near where I was standing. I was frozen solid. He was walking right toward me. My mouth was wide open—completely awestruck— and the towel fell out of my hand. When he got to me, he reached down to pick it up. As he rose and wiped his face, I swear I could hear the music from *2001: A Space Odyssey* playing in my head. There I was, standing thigh-high with my head back as if I was looking up at a skyscraper. As I slowly reached to hand him the water bottle, he said, "Thanks, Josh." I said nothing because I was star struck. Jaden Callahan said my name and I'm on his team? What a day!

That day started a fire in me that was pure. It was a fire that was mine, not my Dad's. Although basketball coaching was his chosen profession, Dad never forced it on me by having me do drills at a young age so I could be the child hoops prodigy that would boost his ego. He let me be a little kid who did little kid things like play with my action figures. He let me come to the game if I wanted to and on my own terms, and I believe that if I had never become interested in basketball, it would have been just fine with him. He would have let me develop my own passion for whatever piqued my interest, and he would've still been my biggest fan, because that's the kind of man he is. He is a father, not a basketball coach, and I am his son, not a basketball player. So beginning on that day, basketball was mine, it was pure, and it was here to stay.

The makings of a hooper

2

A YEAR PASSED, AND I never missed a practice or game for the high school team. I was always in my place on the bench during games with my towels and water bottles ready. My big moment was about to come.

Dad started a Saturday developmental basketball league for kids in grades 1-4. The league focused on teaching fundamentals, but most of all it focused on fun. We would work on dribbling and passing for 30 minutes or so, then get to play games for 20 minutes. My mom was always there, with popsicles ready in case of a boo-boo or meltdown. Nothing heals a 2nd grade injury faster than the icy goodness of a popsicle. The last 10 minutes of the hour we would sit in a circle around Dad. He would review what we had learned, give us some things to work on at home, and celebrate the heck out of our progress. I was one of the few kids who had started practicing my dribbling at home, as well as perfecting my 2nd grade style throw toward the goal. Since I was around the gym literally every day, I was ahead of the curve for 2nd grade hoops.

Dad's 1989 team was a good one. All of the guys grew up playing together and were now seniors. With Jaden leading his band of brothers, we were 20-0 and poised for a run at the state championship. On this night we would face off against Ohio City. Our gym was packed with rowdy fans expecting a replay of the 4 overtime classic that these two teams had played a month before.

I wasn't concerned with any of that though. I was gonna get to play at halftime. Our little developmental league was having a mini game, and I was stoked. This was my big moment. The halftime buzzer sounded, and Dad went into the locker room with the team to make halftime adjustments. Before the game, he had made sure the team video guy would tape the halftime extravaganza so he could watch it when he got home.

As the teams entered their respective locker rooms, I took the floor and put on a dribbling and shooting exhibition... at least in my own mind. We found this archived footage when I was 30 years old, and it did not play out the way I remembered.

Over the span of 8 minutes there were 18 jump

balls, 14 completed passes, 4 kids hit in the face with the ball, and a pair of the most fundamentally solid plays in basketball-hook passes. It had to be hilarious to watch from the stands. But from my perspective, I was 'ballin.' Showing off my newly acquired skills by weaving in and out of traffic with the grace of a mini Isaiah Thomas. The crowd was roaring. In actuality, they were just laughing at our cuteness or talking about the water cooler news of the week. But in my world, it was a Final Four atmosphere.

With the clock winding down, I looked up at the scoreboard with the battle of epic proportions knotted at 0-0. Someone had to make a play, and that someone was going to be me. The ball was thrown to my friend Gavin, who put the ball straight over his head looking like the Statue of Liberty. In predictable fashion, four defenders ran straight to the ball. I WAS WIDE OPEN! I put my hands in the air, doing some sort of jumping jacks, and let out a shrill scream to get Gavin's attention. As the defenders got closer and closer, Gavin started leaning. Before he toppled to the floor, he executed one of the most beautiful hook passes ever attempted. I caught the ball about 12 feet from the basket. That's a long shot for an 8-year-old that weighs 55 pounds soaking wet. I hurled the ball toward the basket with everything I had. I didn't even land on my feet. From my viewpoint on the ground, it seemed like slow motion. The ball was in the air forever and I could hear the *2001: Space Odyssey* music in my head again. SWISH! The crowd goes wild.

I don't remember how the Ohio City game played out. Dad wasn't too concerned with that when we got home. When he was home, he was Dad. When we walked in the door he said, "So let's see the moment everyone has been talking about." He seemed genuinely excited about seeing the tape of me in action. Mom put the tape into the VCR as I sat on the couch, half proud of what I had done and half anticipating what he would say. As the tape rolled we all sat watching the action unfold. He said things like, "Nice pass, Bradley." or "Ooh, that's a big boy rebound by John," and, "I can tell you have been working on your dribbling, Josh." In his subtle way, he always made sure that I understood that basketball was a team game. It was not just about me. The moment finally came when I hit the shot. He let out a yell of celebration. "Yes!" I was grinning from ear to ear and my mom couldn't stop laughing at my graceful landing. When the tape ended, he grabbed me by the shoulders and looked at me straight in the eyes. He did not tell me how great I was. He said something so simple—yet so meaningful. Something that would throw gasoline on my already burning basketball fire… "Josh, I'm so proud of you."

3

IT WAS THE SUMMER of 1989. I was 9 and had just finished the 2nd grade. Life was about to change for the Templeton household. Dad was offered a coaching job at a Christian school called Temple High in Chattanooga, Tennessee. The school was under the umbrella of Dad's college alma mater, Tennessee Temple University. I didn't know anything about Tennessee, but I had no interest in leaving my friends or my comfort zone in Ohio. He drove down for an interview while I stayed home and prayed to the Lord that he would not get the job. The Lord apparently had other plans. So we packed up the truck and headed down south.

Small private schools do not have a reputation for paying their employees well. I didn't realize it then, but it was difficult for my parents to make ends meet for a family of five on Dad's salary and Mom's piano lesson money. We always lived below our means. My 8-year-old sister Rachael, and 4-year-old brother Mitch (aka "Higgs"), and I just thought that was normal living. We didn't know any different. When we took our exit in Chattanooga, Dad drove past housing projects and liquor stores, but all I saw was the rec center, outdoor courts, and ball fields within blocks of our destination. Part of Dad's job package included an old house on the school campus where we could live for free, but there was one catch. The campus was in Highland Park, one of the most notoriously rough areas of Chattanooga. When we arrived at the house on Kirby Avenue we did a walk through before unloading the truck. There was mouse crap everywhere, and roaches scurried across the floor and walls. This place was nasty. It was so bad that Mom sat on the back porch and cried while we started to unload the truck with Dad. The shower and toilet didn't even work for the first two days, so we would have to go down the street to the gym to shower or use the bathroom. While we were unloading the truck, I had to take a dump. I had procrastinated, and this one couldn't wait. So Dad pointed me to the bushes in the back yard and gave me some toilet paper and a shovel. That's how we rolled.

A beautiful thing about children is they don't care

about money, bills, cars, or houses. They are going to just be kids who love life and live for playing—if they are fortunate enough to remain unaware of adult issues. Our financial and bad housing situation was never brought to our attention so we didn't care. Our parents loved each other, and they loved us. We ate and we played, so we were happy as could be—just being kids—and we had no clue discontentment was actually a thing.

4

THE FIRST YEAR AT Temple was a challenge for Dad. It was a transition year. The administration had decided it was time to make the move from the TACS (the small Christian school athletic league in Tennessee) to the TSSAA (the public school athletic association of Tennessee), so Temple would be competing against the big boys now. Dad inherited a team that was much more heart than athleticism and talent. This made it tough, considering the insanely high level of athleticism and talent in our new league, District 4A. But Dad loved a challenge. He lived for the process of building a program with a culture that could make its mark on the state; by being the embodiment of everything that is right in high school sports.

By Dad's second year at Temple High, people around town started to take notice of the small Christian school from the inner city. We didn't have a starter over 6'2" but we played hard and played together. I say 'we,' because I considered myself part of the team. I would faithfully reside in my usual spot on the bench, handing out water and towels to my new heroes. In district play we reeled off 7 straight wins after trailing at half. The last of which was on the road against perennial power City High School, led by 6'7" All-State forward Ara Matthews.

Ara was an incredible talent as well as a trash talker extraordinaire. He was known around town as 'the Sultan of Smack,' for both his impeccable timing as a shot blocker, and his affinity for verbal abuse. We were down 6 at halftime. Our players were warming up in front of our bench when Ara casually strolled through our shooting lines. His angry eyes fixed on our version of 'The Round Mound of Rebound,' our 6'1" post player, Terry Buckner. When they made eye contact, Matthews spit the single cleverest line of trash talk I have ever heard. "On this day, ye shall lose." I think Terry was okay, but I pissed my pants. Actually, I know Terry was okay, because on that day, we did not lose. We took the lead for the first time with 1:00 left in the 3rd quarter on a put back by Terry. We never looked back as we methodically ran our offense and frustrated City High to the point that they resorted to gambling on defense. This led to many easy back-door layups that turned out to be the difference in the game.

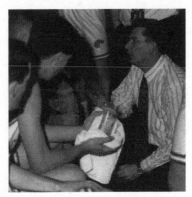

Dad giving instructions during a timeout

The next Friday we played the Patriots of Chattanooga School for the Arts and Sciences. This was a big one. If we were the new mutts in the kennel, Arts and Sciences were the pure bred pit bulls. These guys were bad to the bone, and to this day they are arguably the best team the city of Chattanooga has ever seen. Their starting lineup consisted of 6'7" George Hudgins (who played a key role in Drexel's amazing 96-19 run over the span of his 4-year career), 6'6" Holy Cross standout Carlos Clark, 6'3" dynamic guard Phillip Moss (who possibly could have been the best of them all if he had been academically eligible for college), 6'1" JUCO signee Carlos Pride, and, their main man, 6'3" Porter Roberts (4-year starter at Purdue when Glenn "Big Dog" Robinson played. Porter is ranked #25 on Bleacher Reports top 50 Purdue basketball players of all time.)

It was a game of tempo, and our methodical pace frustrated the high flying Patriots. Terry Buckner was at it again, battling it out with Clark and Hudgins in the post. We went into the locker room at half with a six-point lead, and the buzz in the Vance Gym was electric. Could this really happen? Could we take down the best in our first year in the league?

Arts came out of the half with a furious press in their attempt to get the tempo of the game in their favor. It shook our guys a little but never broke them. The game stayed nip and tuck until Porter Roberts drained a 3 with 22 seconds left to take the lead, and then we turned the ball over on our next possession, forcing us to foul Roberts. Like big time players do, Roberts calmly stepped to the line and knocked down both free throw attempts. With only seven seconds remaining, we had one more chance to tie the game, but our 3-point attempt came up short and we lost by 3. The next day, the newspaper ran a story about the game calling our team "the new kid in town." People around school were excited. Everyone loves a good underdog story anyway, so naturally, in only the second year of Dad's tenure, our program had intrigued basketball fans around the city.

5

MEANWHILE IN MY BASKETBALL world, I was starting to get better. Dad gave me drills to work on my ball handling. I was in the 3rd grade now and was still throwing the ball toward the basket like a shot put. Dad knew if I was going to develop properly, I would have to stop chucking it from the hip, so he enlisted the help of Tennessee Temple University coach Tim Collins, who was an expert in the science of shooting the basketball. His son Nathan was thirteen and had one of the sweetest 7th grade strokes in town, and as luck would have it, his youngest daughter Chantel was beginning to play the piano. Since we didn't have any money, Dad made Coach Collins an offer. The offer was to trade piano lessons for Chantel from Mom, in exchange for shooting lessons for me from Coach Collins. He agreed. Coach Collins didn't just go through the motions either, taking my 3rd grade shot development seriously. It was a pretty impressive testament to his character considering the fact that he was a college coach making time for a 3rd grade kid.

Looking back, this was the point in my life where I went from being a little fan who was excited about basketball, to a little player who was realizing that the sky was the limit. It was an exciting time. I took every bit of the instruction I received from Coach Collins as gospel. If he wanted me to move my shooting pocket, I did. If he wasn't happy with my follow through or foot-work, I tried over and over again until I got it right. He was strict about the technique, and I was all in. As I got better, I practiced more on my own, and during this time, I had an 'aha' moment. It was a simple yet profound truth that became a defining reason for my innate desire to work on my game. MAKING SHOTS IS A RIDICULOUS AMOUNT OF FUN! The more I could make—the more I wanted to make. It was like a drug, and I was addicted. I was getting exponentially better with every passing week. Every shot I made be-came fuel that was added to my basketball fire.

I can see now that Dad was blessed with the gift of foresight. He had obviously spent a great deal of time contemplating how to coach your kid, and had sought out some pretty solid advice from experienced coaches that he trusted. He had a remarkable grasp on the fact that, if we were going to maintain the healthy father-son relationship that we had, he would have to delegate a good deal of my coaching and development to some trusted experts, so I could be constantly hearing a fresh voice. Tim Collins was the first expert he recruited, and he turned out to be a game changer.

6

DURING THE SUMMER OF 1991 before my 5th grade year, we exchanged our old roach motel for a bigger roach motel a few blocks from campus. It was an old two story upgrade with a tree house and basketball hoop in the back yard. Rachael, Higgs, and I couldn't wait to get in that back yard and wreck shop all day long. How this upgrade came about was actually a unique situation.

Darin Martin was Dad's starting point guard. After turning heads during his junior season, he was poised for an even bigger senior year. The surprising finish the team had last year had everyone amped for the new season. We had two big rising sophomore forwards in 6'5" Karl Lewis and Andy Cash who grew 3 inches over the summer and was now standing at 6'8" tall. They were ready for varsity prime time. Darin was the perfect seasoned point guard to lead our mixed bag of young talent and solid upperclassman in our quest to win our first district championship. Except, there was one problem. In early June, Darin's father had taken a job in Charlotte, North Carolina. Dad was sure that Darin was gone, and he was preparing as such. It looked like we would have somewhat of a developmental year with so many young players and no point guard to lead them, but Darin wasn't havin' it.

Darin objected so adamantly about leaving his teammates and going to a new school for his senior year that his parents came up with a proposition for Dad. If he would let Darin stay at our house as a temporary member of our family for this school year, they would let us live in their big (to us at least) old house during the year for an absurdly low rent. Mom was always ready to bolt from the dilapidated house on Kirby, so she jumped at the opportunity for the cheap upgrade on Duncan.

It was an easy decision for my parents. Dad loved all his players like sons, so it was not much of a stretch for him to bring one into his home, especially one of Darin's character. He was a model student who was kind to everyone he came in contact with. His coaches and teachers loved him, his peers respected him, and the youngins wanted to be him. Best of all, he was going to be my new roommate. I had always been the big brother, and now I would get to have a big brother for the first time in my life.

Our families made the agreement, and we moved in. Darin's daily life had an immediate impact on me. To this day, he was probably the most disciplined teenager I have seen in my entire life. Our first morning in the house, I woke up to the sound of a basketball bouncing outside of the window of our second floor room. I proceeded to wipe the sleep out of my eyes and stumble to the window to see what my new big bro was up to. I looked out and saw him down there, already soaked in sweat, getting in some serious game speed work. I just watched in amazement. I had never seen someone practice at game speed on their own. He was working uncomfortably fast. It planted another seed in my mind, and I remember thinking, *so that's how you get good like Darin.* He also had a nightly habit of pumping off one hundred push-ups and one hundred sit-ups before bed. Sometimes, if I wasn't too sleepy (this dude would get up early), I would join him in the mornings and rebound for him. He had an amazing influence on my work ethic and even convinced me to start my own nightly push-up and sit-up routine that would stick with me until my college career ended. When he would finish his morning workout, I would stay outside and mimic his workout and all his moves.

7

IT WAS SEPTEMBER OF 1991. Basketball season was creeping up on us and we were all ready for the season to begin. There was no football at Temple High because we didn't have enough boys in the high school to field a capable team. Temple High folks anticipated basketball season like Roll Tiders anticipate the 3rd Saturday in August. I had been working diligently on my ball handling drills from Dad, my new shot—designed by Coach Collins—and the game speed workouts that I copied from Darin. My shooting ability was starting to take off and set me apart from the other kids. Dad never pushed me to go outside and play. He didn't have to. Sure, I played my share of Nintendo. I still took the Bengals to the Tecmo Super Bowl and laid Mike Tyson on the virtual canvas like other kids my age, but the idea of a perfect day to me was to go outside and play ball. I made a lot of 'baller' friends around the neighborhood. We would organize some epic tackle football games, and basketball games went down on the outdoor courts or at the rec center on the regular.

No matter what your age, if you go outside to play ball with the neighborhood kids of Highland Park, you had better learn to be hard or stay inside. Staying inside was not an option for me, I was an outdoor soul so I had no choice. Bloody noses, scrapes, scratches, and the occasional brouhaha were the price of play on the outdoor confines. Respect was never given... you had to earn it. Since I was always small for my age, I had developed somewhat of a little man complex. I wasn't going to do much damage with my fists if the moment called for me to throw them, so I had to earn my keep with my game. And that's what I did, becoming Chattanooga's own 11-year-old Billy Hoyle.

The first time I rolled into the East Lake Rec Center to play, a few of the boys chuckled when I walked in the door with my ball tucked under my arm. There were 11 boys ages 10-15 in the gym, so a pick-up game was bound break out. Two of the older boys started to pick teams and, of course, I was the only kid not picked up. But that would be a mistake that the kids would make only once. I had next, and when I got on the court, I rained 3's like it was 2016.

Once the boys got savvy to what I could do, they would use me as a hustle to stack their team. I was just happy I got to play. This newly acquired skill felt good. Sometimes, the older and bigger boys would get a bit salty since I wasn't supposed to be able to play looking like I did. I got roughed up a few times, but backing down was not gonna happen, and the boys respected that. My game started to get more respectable with each passing week.

Unbeknownst to me at the time, Dad was always assisting me in my travail toward hardness. He knew I would have to be hard. He knew where we lived, what I liked to do, and the boys I would be playing with. He also knew that my size would always make it an uphill battle. He was a disciplinarian, but I wouldn't say he was strict, just hard. I was always a little rowdy, but I knew that if I was actin' a fool, there would be a reckoning; and there often was.

He did a few little things here and there that—looking back—I can now see were obviously calculated moves. Dad was an avid boxing fan. I was, and still am, as well. One Friday Dad came home from practice with two pairs of boxing gloves. He told me that he was going to face off against me in our living room version of Friday night fights. I was jacked and couldn't wait to show Dad my jab, or to dance around like Evander Holyfield. He had Mom, Rachael, and Higgs sit on the couch to judge the fight. The gloves were too small for his hands so he held them, hitting me with slap shots and jabs. I went at him hard while he rang my bell many times.

I remember my ears ringing, and Mom saying, "Kevin, you are hitting him too hard."

He turned to tell her, "No, he's fine. This is a good fi—"

Before he could get the word out, I came in with an overhand right cheap shot that would make Floyd Mayweather proud.

He then said to Mom in disgust, "See Vicky, he's fine."

When you are my size, you quickly learn to master the art of the sucker punch.

If there was a fight on pay per view, he was on it, and the entire team would come over. On the night of the first Evander Holyfield vs. Riddick "Big Daddy" Bowe fight, we had the team over to the Duncan house to watch. I had a neighborhood 'baller' friend named Ronnie, and his mom also had some friends over for a barbecue in their front yard across the street. As the uneventful preliminary bouts were taking place, the party across the street was getting raucous. The sounds of arguing and bedlam were starting to carry over the loud music at Ronnie's house, and the noise made its way across the street into our living room. A few of the guys started to file out onto the front porch to see what all the hullabaloo was about.

Within minutes, sophomore guard Mark Chambers peeked inside and said, "Guys, y'all might want to come check this out. The better fight is across the street."

Everybody filed out to the front porch (some of them literally eating popcorn) to catch the action. Ronnie's mom was having a disagreement with a man. For some reason, everyone in the front yard was trying to calm her down at the same time, which only escalated the situation. At one point, there were 10-15 people in their yard all yelling expletives at each other at the same time. Ronnie's mom yelled over the crowd, "I ain't gonna take this." She proceeded to walk toward the man swinging an old broom by the brush end. At this point Dad yelled into the house to get Mom to call the cops before someone got killed. This lady came in with a barrage attack laying the wood on this poor guy. He was covering up while she was firing head shots, body shots, and shots to the nether regions, until finally she broke the broom stick over his head! He quickly grabbed the shard of broomstick, and, in a moment of rage, stabbed her in the leg with it.

Then it got ugly.

She screamed bloody murder, stumbled, then slowly rose to her feet and went at him with kamikaze velocity while beating this guy bloody. At this point, every player on the porch had popcorn, and a few were placing bets. All hell was breaking loose. Ronnie's front yard turned into a mini colosseum of pure unadulterated mayhem, where every person in the yard was engaged in some form of hand to hand combat. The whole ordeal lasted about five minutes and then the cops showed up. That was our queue to go back inside and watch the fight.

Holyfield/Bowe 1 would go down in boxing history as one of the greatest fights of all time. It is debated that round 10 was the greatest round of all time. But in our book, it was the second best fight of the night. It had nothing on the 'Thrilla by the Grilla.'

8

PRETTY MUCH EVERY DAY, Darin got the keys to the gym from Dad and went by himself to hone his skills. He got the keys under one condition: he could only turn on the balcony lights. Did I mention that small private schools are cheap? Usually, I would tag along. The Duncan House was five blocks from the gym, so Darin would often drive Dad's beat up 1982 Mercury Cougar, affectionately known as 'the Coog.' That car was a work of art. Brown and rusty from the Ohio salt, you couldn't tell the where the nasty paint job ended and the rust began. It even did that nasty 80's car thing where the cloth ceiling comes unattached and is just hanging down tickling your head. 'The Coog' was the first of many legendary cars that became a trademark of the Templeton family.

The Vance Gym was an old aluminum gymnasium

that seated around 1400. There was no air conditioning, so in the hot months the aluminum would magnify the heat like an oven. Everyone called it the Hot Box. The weather forecasters could call for temperatures upwards of 95 degrees, but it would be 10-20 degrees hotter in the Hot Box. You would have to go outside to cool off. The place just felt like work. It was hard as a coffin nail and was a perfect fit for the mentality of the culture that Dad was building at Temple.

On one particular Saturday in October, Darin did his game speed workout on one end, and I shot on the other. After our workouts, he was getting a few extra shots while I went outside for a minute to cool off. When I came back in, Darin was still shooting on the far end. That is when I got the best/worst idea of my young life.

I walked up to Darin and said, "Hey Darin, you should try to dunk off one of those folding chairs. I bet you could get your elbows above the rim."

Yeah, I said that. I'm not sure if Darin took it as a challenge or if he just was being nice, because that's the kind of guy he was.

"You think? Sure, I'll try it. Go grab a chair," he said.

I was about to burst with excitement. *This is gonna be so awesome,* is what I thought to myself as I ran to get the chair.

Darin measured up the chair and put it exactly where he wanted it.

He looked at me and said, "Alright now, hold it tight so it doesn't move when I jump off."

I was so pumped I couldn't even speak. He dribbled back to near half court and started running toward the chair, carefully measuring his steps. I could hear that stupid *Space Odyssey* music again, and was so excited I think I completely forgot about my chair holding responsibilities. My hands were now effectively resting on the chair. When his foot hit the chair, the music came to a screeching stop. The chair went sailing toward the baseline bleachers slamming into them with a loud crash, and Darin fell back, feet over his head, and landed on his right wrist.

I stood there in horror, watching him roll on the ground clutching his wrist. I can honestly say that I hadn't been this afraid since I snuck out of bed to catch a peek at *Pet Sematary* during Mom and Dad's movie night. The sick thing is, I wasn't even worried about Darin at all.

Dad is gonna kill me, I thought to myself.

"Your dad is gonna kill me," Darin said.

Oh okay. Yeah. That's better. You definitely should take the blame for this one. I'm just an idiot kid, and you should know better. But the only thing I could muster up to say was, "Are you okay?"

Yeah, I'm perfect. The bone in my wrist is sticking straight out and I can't feel anything below my elbow. Should be able to walk it off, Darin probably thought.

"Yeah. It doesn't look good, but I'll live," Darin said, his voice shaky from the pain.

We gathered our gear and hopped in 'the Coog.' I was crying at this point and Darin—being Darin—was trying to console me. He reached under the wheel with his left hand and put the car into gear in one of the most awkward driving moves ever pulled off.

Those five blocks felt like a cross-country trip. When we went in the house I was literally hiding behind Darin.

Darin, staring at his shoes, said, "Coach, I messed up." He lifted his arm to show him the damage.

Dad didn't even hesitate. "Well, let's head to the E.R. and get this thing taken care of." He was so cool under pressure.

9

THE 1991-1992 BASKETBALL SEASON was officially underway. Darin's wrist was healing nicely, and it looked like he would be making his season debut in mid-December. This year had the potential to be a breakout year for our program as well as our culture. Darin would be leading a big, talented group of freshman and sophomores through the brutal District 4A schedule, and in the meantime, I was chomping at the bit, ready for my 5th grade season. The fun factor of the game had been amplified so much now that I had a real big boy shot. I played in an elementary school league for 5th and 6th graders against a few players I'd be doing battle with for the next 8 years. I no longer sat on the bench and handed out water for Dad's team because I had my own basketball schedule now and would miss too many games.

Our team seemed to be the real deal this year. When the game turned into a blowout, which it often did, I would recruit kids from other schools to go upstairs to the wrestling mats in the balcony of the Vance Gym that overlooked the basketball court. We would play tackle football or American eagle (the tackle version of the child's game red-rover). A few times one of us would throw an errant pass that would fly down onto the court. The ref would blow the whistle to stop the action and the Temple player closest to the football would launch it back up to the balcony without hesitation. Many Chattanooga high school basketball rivalries began on those wrestling mats.

One in particular was my rivalry with Keith Galloway who was an early bloomer and already an all-around great athlete. He was also the son of Joe Galloway, one of the most well respected coaches in the district. Our fathers were cut from the same cloth of culture connoisseurs and had developed a friendship since we had moved down from Ohio. Keith was a great out of school friend. He even had my back when I landed my first haymaker in a childhood scrap versus one of his classmates during the varsity game at their place. We always bonded at the high school games but competed like wild animals when we played against each other. In early February of my 5th grade season we faced off in the elementary championship game.

The day of my championship game, Dad was taking the varsity team on the road to play South Pittsburg. When he dropped me off at school he told me to come by the gym after school before they left for the game. When I walked into the gym with my buddies, he peeked out of his office and called for me to come in. I was nervous about the game. I know it was the fifth grade, but it was the biggest game of my young life and I had never played in a championship game before. All these feelings were new to me.

I guess Dad already knew this.

"You ready?" He asked.

"Yessir."

"I hate that I'm going to miss the best game you've played yet," he said.

I laughed.

"Are you nervous?"

"Not really." I was totally posing.

"Good. There is never a reason to be nervous when you get a chance to have as much fun as you're about to have. I mean... playing in your first championship game against Galloway," he said, as I grinned from ear to ear. "Y'all are gonna go to battle. Regardless of who wins, the fun is in the battle for guys like us. I can't wait to watch the tape when I get home. Now go out there and let it all hang out."

I floated out of that office feeling like I could take on the armies of Sparta with a weapon crafted by MacGyver.

The game was a battle, as far as elementary championships go, but they got the best of us by 4 points. Keith hit 5 threes and had 26 points. The pregame talk with Dad had me playing pretty loose. The pressure is non-existent when you are reminded about how much fun it is just to compete. I dropped 32 and hit 6 threes.

Dad got the call about the game on the way home. A little birdie told me later, that after he hung up with Mom, he had a smile on his face the entire way home and didn't say a word.

Dad's program at Temple made great strides in 91-92. The culture he had been working so hard to cultivate was becoming a reality. Led by Darin, our Crusaders had a huge year. They won the school's first ever District 4A and Region 2A championships. We pounded Oakdale 74-52 in the sub-state game in front of a packed Vance Gym crowd. Three years after Dad took the helm, Temple High would be making their very first state tournament appearance in school history, drawing East Robertson in the first round. We led 14-12 at the end of the first quarter, but Brandon Rippey came off the bench for East Robertson, and spelled doom for our championship hopes. He scored 17 in the first half alone, going 3-4 from beyond the arc, boosting them to a 38-28 lead going into halftime. In the second half, David Woodard, East Robertson's sensational junior All-State performer, took over, electrifying the crowd with some highlight reel dunks. He scored 23 in the second half and 30 for the game, and they went on to win 82-66. Our season would end at 27-7. Despite the disappointing finish, it was a big year for the program.

Darin taking it to the rack in the Sub-state game vs. Oakdale

10

EVERYONE AROUND THE SCHOOL was on a basketball high from our first ever state tournament run. The basketball culture Dad had been building for the last 3 years was as strong as it had ever been, and our teams had become known for our solid half court pressure defense. With Andy defending the rim, we were very hard to score on. With the graduation of Darin, we were going to be green at the guard spots in the upcoming year. But with Andy and Karl on the front line, we would be a team to watch again in the brutal District 4A. The summer would be important for the development of our sophomore guards, sharp shooter Nick Shiraef and bad boy Mark Chambers.

Darin went off to college, so our 'housing for adopted son' arrangement had run its course, and we had to move again. The church had a tiny 3 bedroom, 1 bath house across the street from the gym, with a mini parking lot next to it where they would park buses. Dad made a deal with the pastor that let us stay there for $200 per month. I couldn't have been happier with the move, because it was like I had my own gym in the backyard. Nick lived across the street from us and he took Darin's place as my new shooting partner. A few weeks after we moved in, we realized that we didn't even need to ask Dad for the keys anymore. You could just go to the back door and kick the bottom, and it would just pop open. GAME ON! I don't know how many shots we got up in the Hot Box that off-season, but I can guarantee it was more than 75,000 each.

To make extra money, Dad ran a little kid's basketball camp every summer that taught basic fundamentals through fun, competitive games to the elementary tykes hungry for ball. From 9-11am, we would have 1st through 3rd graders. He used me for skill demonstrations and to teach the younger ones. He said, "If you teach it, you will be better at it." This turned out to be true. I think of the wise words of Salvador Dali, "Thoughts become unclouded when they pass through the lips and the fingertips." After the babies left, it was time for the big boys to play. The 4-7th graders got to work on their skills and play competitive games from 12-3pm.

At this point, I was so far ahead of everyone in this

age group that Dad couldn't even stack the teams against me when it was time to play games. I didn't care though. I had my heart set on winning the camper of the week trophy that Dad gave away on the last day of camp. I had never won it before, but I knew this year was different and I was not going to be denied. I played circles around everyone all week.

When you are a child, trophies are a big deal. I guess some people never grow out of that, which is why many coach's offices you walk into are like personal shrines to themselves. Dad was different though. He had a higher calling. The TSSAA state coach of the year plaque he won the year before wasn't hanging in his office. Instead, it had found its way into one of his dresser drawers. The culture he was building at Temple was about team, celebration of others, humility, and shared success. He would be the first one to model this mentality every single day, because he was the champion of our culture.

But, I was still an 11-year-old kid, and I wanted that trophy. I knew I was going to get it. I felt like I had made it obvious enough for Dad, so he wouldn't catch any flak from a salty parent who said he just wanted to give it to his son. When it came time for the closing camp ceremonies, Dad set up a table with some trophies and t-shirts on it. Everyone had their name called to come up and shake his hand and get their t-shirt. He would then announce the most improved boy and girl players of the week. My friend Joel Money, who lived a few blocks down and ran with me from court to court outside during the last 3 summers, won the boys most improved award. I was so happy for him and gave him a high five as he sat back down beside me wearing the silliest 'trying not to grin' look on his face.

"And the boy's camper of the week goes to..."

I started to stand up.

"Jeff Carter."

I awkwardly sat back down and clapped with a 'trying not to frown' smile on my face.

Dad didn't raise a pouter, but I was a little kid, and this time I couldn't help myself. He raised me to celebrate the achievements of others. Jeff came back smiling and I gave him a high five too, but I couldn't completely hide my disappointment. Sometimes, it's really hard to be a great teammate, even when you know you should, especially when you're 11 years old.

Dad knew that a lesson on the meaninglessness of a painted gold piece of plastic was more important than my need for some validation. But there was even more to it than that. He wanted me to be the best TEAMMATE I could be. He wanted me to be a true leader who had the whole package. He always had reasons for the things he did.

After we racked the balls and turned off the lights, Dad reached in his pocket and handed me an envelope with 'J.T.' written on the front. As I took it from his hand, he said, "Open it before you go to sleep tonight."

"Okay Dad, thanks." I said, as we started to make our short walk home.

I couldn't wait to read it. I rushed through my dinner and told Mom and Dad I was really tired from camp.

"Well I think I'm gonna read and go to bed. Goodnight Mom. Goodnight Dad," I said.

Dad looked at me with confusion because he knew getting me to read a book was like pulling teeth. Not only that, it was only 7pm!

"Okay Josh, Love you. Sleep good," Mom said.

Finally, I climbed into the rack and opened the letter. It was hand written and read:

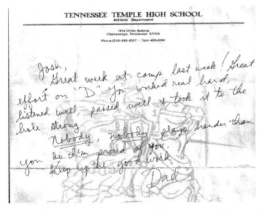

In that moment, I could not have cared less about a

stupid trophy. *Dad said nobody plays harder than me, and 'nobody' was written twice and underlined twice, so he must've really meant it,* I thought as I stared at the ceiling with a satisfied smile on my face.

I didn't realize then what I do now. I was a great shooter for my age. I may have even been the best in town, but he didn't mention that. He wanted me to be the most complete player I could be, as well as make my teammates better, and he highlighted the other aspects of my game that I did well. He knew that I took his word as the infallible truth, and by reading this, I would take more pride in being a player than being a shooter. I believe that he intentionally put it in my mind that nobody played harder than I did. Eleven-year-old minds are easily shaped by the people they respect and seek approval from, and that one sentence became my identity for the rest of my career. *Nobody, nobody plays harder than me.*

5th grade hoops

11

6TH GRADE. WE WERE the big dogs in the elementary school now, and I was ready to show off all the work I had done that summer. The players in the NBA were wearing those stupid spandex under daisy duke shorts. I had to wear that too, and somehow convinced my mom to take me to the local sporting goods store to get a pair. There was one problem. I weighed about 80 pounds and my legs were skinny as a rail. I tried on the smallest size, and they were still loose on my thighs. I still thought I looked like an NBA 'baller.' In retrospect, I looked like a clown, but so did everyone else.

Meanwhile, the neighborhood was getting rougher. Our tackle football games got shut down by some concerned parents, mine included, on account of a few broken arms and a broken nose.

Mom was getting tired of worrying, and started looking for reasons to move.

Strike one:

On a Sunday morning in September, Dad got robbed at gunpoint while walking from our house to church. I thought it was ironic that the muggers stole his Bible and his wallet, but it obviously wasn't their first rodeo. Where else would a good church man keep that tithe check envelope?

Strike two:

Halloween was getting wilder too. Trick or Treating after dark was no longer an option. On Halloween night, our doorbell rang around 9:30pm. Dad answered the door, and there stood a 6'5" grown man holding out a black garbage bag. He looked pretty intimidating, wearing a trench coat and sporting a full beard.

"Trick or treat man," he said, in a bellowing voice.

Dad peered into his bag. There was a small TV, a ton of VHS tapes, CD's, and a few watches. Without hesitation, and being the cool cat under pressure that he was, Dad said, "Hang on a second." He went over to our makeshift entertainment center and grabbed a handful of VHS movies and CD's.

"Happy Halloween," he said, as he dropped the booty into the bag.

"Thanks man. Happy Halloween," the trick or treater said, as he walked off the porch.

Strike 3:

Our car got stolen out of the bus lot beside the house for the 3rd time in 4 months. The police always found it a day or two later abandoned on the side of the road somewhere. I guess somebody just really liked 'the Coog,' and had to take it on periodical joy rides. This time, the damage was irreparable, and 'the Coog' had given up the ghost. Mom was about to go to the grocery store when she went outside and saw that 'the Coog' was gone. She walked back in the house with the most dejected look on her face and said, "We gotta move."

She didn't even know about the worst incident that Nick and I protected like a matter of national security. Every other day or so Mom would ask me to go to the gym and fill our cooler with ice from the ice machine. It was a one block trip that usually took around two hours. Mom knew this, so if she needed the ice by dinner time, she would ask me to go around 3:00. I would hop up, grab Dad's keys, and round up Joel or Nick to get some shots up. That day it was Nick.

Vance gym was a little bit like the 'Field of Dreams' in that, 'if you open it, they will come.' But this day it got a little out of hand. Before we knew it, we had about 14 guys of all ages in the gym ready to hoop. Naturally, a pick-up game broke out. There was a guy there named Carlos that everybody called 'Big 'Los.' He was big but incredibly soft.

There was an unwritten law for the pick-up games in the Vance gym—the defense calls fouls, but you must respect the game. It kept the games fast paced, minimized whining, and fit with the culture of who we were at Temple. If you needed to call a foul, you were probably making a soft move. During the third game of the day, 'Big 'Los' took the ball up after an offensive rebound and called foul. Nick ignored him, grabbed the ball off the rim and headed the other way. As did everyone else who knew how pick-up was played at Vance. 'Big 'Los' proceeded to walk back down the floor to the defensive end, mumbling expletives under his breath. On the next possession, 'Big 'Los' got the ball underneath and was hacked on principle. He looked straight up at the ceiling, walked off the floor and reached into his bag. He stood up and walked back toward the court brandishing a piece that would make Dirty Harry Callahan proud. One of the players yelled "Gun!" and everyone in the gym scattered like the roaches in our kitchen when I turned on the lights to get my midnight snack. Nick and I got out of there so fast, the ball may have still been bouncing in the empty gym as Nick and I were sitting in my room. He looked at me with disbelief and said, "What just happened?" I just sat there stunned and silent, and thought to myself, *we gotta move.* We never spoke of the phenomenon again.

We won the elementary championship that year and I accomplished a feat that no 6th grader had ever done before, (as far as I know). I made a half-court shot and scored on the other team's basket in the same season.

The varsity team finished the season 24-8 that year. They were eliminated in the regional semifinals by a good Chattanooga Christian team. Throughout the grueling District 4A schedule, our sophomore guards gained valuable experience. Fueled by the bitterness of the CCS defeat, our guys were committed to getting better over the summer to make next year the year of the Crusader. Andy and Karl would be seniors, and Nick and Chambers were now ready for prime time.

Andy Cash

12

MY GRANDPA WAS A baptist pastor in Ohio, but he and Grandma wanted to move closer to us so they could be involved in the lives of their grandchildren. Dad had the bright idea that they should buy a house together since we couldn't afford anything decent on our own. Grandpa must have liked the idea because he resigned from his church, accepted a teaching position at Tennessee Temple University Seminary, and packed up the truck to head down south. Mom and Dad took us to go see the new house we would live in. It was a 4 bedroom, 3 bath place in the suburbs, and was a mansion compared to what we had been used to. Best of all—NO ROACHES! We were beside ourselves about our new house, especially Mom. The neighborhood was nice, but I worried that there wouldn't be many 'ballers' to hoop with me outside.

Having my grandparents in the house was nice. We got to see them every day, and Grandma had some of the best home cooking in the country. Players from our team would frequent our house on a regular basis and often invited themselves, because they knew full well that Grandma would serve them up a succulent meal. The more she cooked for the guys, the more the guys would randomly show up. Dad liked having them over too, since he built trust with his players by opening his home to them. Everyone knew they were welcome to come hang out and get a home cooked meal anytime they wanted. Dad's players weren't just chess pieces Dad would move around the board. They were part of our family. The only thing Grandma liked more than seeing people throw down her food was the basketball games, and she and Grandpa never missed a game. She would get dressed up for each game in her Sunday best, lived and died with every play, and was known for her patented double fist pump. After big wins, they would wait in the living room for me and Dad to get home, so we could all relive the big plays. It was fun to share these moments with them.

That spring was when I chose to specialize in basketball. At first, I loved playing soccer, but I slowly began to lose interest because I kept sticking my face in the path of a booted ball, and that got old fast. I also played baseball until my 7th grade year. Dad played baseball in college, and I'm sure he would have liked to see me develop an interest in the game. I enjoyed my time on the diamond, but always found myself counting down the outs until I could get outta there and get to a hoop to get some shots up. Maybe the game was a little too slow for my taste. I didn't become a basketball-only player until I was in seventh grade. As hard as Dad tried to get me into other sports, my heart belonged to basketball. Basketball was just who I was, and he let me be who I was.

13

OUR FIRST MORNING IN the new house, I woke up to a familiar sound. Bounce, bounce, bounce, swish, bounce, bounce, bounce, boing. I sat straight up in bed, thinking, *someone is hoopin.* I threw on my clothes and walked out the back door. All I could see were trees behind our house, but I could hear that ball bouncing away. I looked down the hill to the corner of our back yard where there was a small opening between the house one street down from ours and the woods. I walked toward the hoop sounds coming from the opening. I was getting warmer. This was the most exciting game of Marco Polo I had ever played. I came out the other side of the opening and saw Tripp Ransom working on his game. He had a flat driveway with a lane and 3-point arc painted on it. His goal had a square backboard and was solidly built into the ground. The best part of it was he had some game. I walked toward him with a skip in my step.

"Hey, I'm Josh. Can I shoot with ya?"

"Ya man. I'm Tripp."

We got to know each other and shot around until lunch time. I thought he looked familiar, and come to find out, we had played against each other. He played for a Catholic school named O.L.P.H., which was in our elementary league. Tripp and I had faced off against each other three times during my 5th grade year. He seemed as hungry to get better at basketball as I was. I couldn't believe it—I had done the impossible. I found a real 'hooper' in suburbia.

That summer Dad was going to send me to the legendary Don Meyer's basketball camp at David Lipscomb University. It was a week-long individual boarding camp that cost $300 per camper. Word on the street had it as the best individual skill development camp in the southeast. Dad told me he would send me if I did some work to help pay for it. I was in. It wasn't hard to talk Tripp into going to Lipscomb's camp with me either. I also invited him to play with my middle school team at Tennessee Temple University's team camp. He was a basketball junkie just like me.

Don Meyer and company were the next group of experts Dad had recruited to play a role in my development. Dad had done his due diligence researching who had the best skills camp. This place was a real 'hooper's' dream. These guys were as serious about the game as me and Tripp were. Every night we got to sit on the sidelines and watch the David Lipsomb University Bisons go through an entire collegiate practice run by Don Meyer and his staff. It was an up close and personal courtside view of the intensity and speed of college basketball. I was also introduced to William James, who is now one of my favorite philosophers of all time. I etched his quote *'As you think so shall you be,'* in big block letters on the cover of my notebook.

We went home with a toolbox of new drills, sharpened skills, and some new tricks of the trade. My notebook was filled with pages upon pages of golden nuggets of basketball wisdom that I would review for years to come. It became an integral part of my basketball persona. Anything I learned about the game at any time, I wrote in this book. It also became a daily chronicle of my career. By the end of my basketball career, I had stacks of notebooks in a box filled with golden nuggets of wisdom from great coaches and players, including stories, learning experiences, setbacks, mental challenges, and processes of improvement, all gathered over my entire playing career. As Jim Rohn said, "A life worth living is a life worth recording."

The next week was team camp. My school team of 7th and 8th graders was looking pretty strong, thanks to a few new kids whose parents wanted them to play for Dad. The best of which was rising 8th grade man-child Gabe Johnson. Gabe and his older brother A.J. came from a small Christian elementary school in Lookout Valley. We played against them in our elementary league. Braucht Walters was a fiery rising 8th grade guard from Pennsylvania whose father had just taken a job at the University. Another 8th grader was Ricky Gossett. He was a long, lanky 6'1" forward who looked exactly like Shaggy from Scooby Doo, but was a tough, blue collar kid who was much more athletic than he appeared. Me and my Highland Park running mate Joel Money held down the 7th grade class.

For the next two weeks, it was our group from school, savvy guard Dave Dalton (the son of Marc Dalton—Dad's best friend and coaching colleague from Ohio), and Tripp, who I was trying to get to talk his parents into sending him to Temple so he could play with us in high school. Dad told us at open gym before the week started that we had better bring our hard hats, because we would be playing up with all 9th and 10th graders.

Our rising freshman class was loaded. They were led by Danny Deas. Deas was a ridiculous athlete who might have been better at baseball than he was at basketball. His other classmates were smooth point guard Jeremy Kennedy, Gabe's brother A.J., 6'6" Joey Cash (Andy's brother), bruising big man Aaron McGuirt, and guards Matt Neal and Brent Mink. Seven good players in one class was rare at our school, considering that each class had no more than 15 boys, and Dad was very excited about the talent in this group.

Dad would split his varsity and junior varsity teams up into 4 teams. They would all play on the varsity level during the week. The sophomores through seniors would be split into 3 teams. This left the freshmen (Deas & Co.) competing against varsity teams on their own. He knew he would need a few of the freshman to step up and compete for varsity minutes, so his plan was to throw them to the wolves so he would see who could rise to the occasion.

Dad's plate would be full during the week because he would be coaching all 4 high school teams at camp, as well as running coach's clinics during the week. He was always preparing for the future of the program and felt that there was something special about the toughness of my middle school group, so he had devised a plan. He would recruit a specialist to coach us for the week. A coach that embodied the culture he was building, that had a high basketball I.Q., as well as a certain level of hardness that would push this little group of psychos to be even crazier. A coach who loved defense and warrior culture. So much so that—if he coached these pups for one week—he might get hooked and come along for the entire ride. Enter Lefty Glascock.

14

LEFTY GLASCOCK PLAYED BASKETBALL and baseball for Tennessee Temple University in the early 70's. After college he had a cup of coffee in minor league baseball before deciding to get married and become a college basketball coach. From 1975-1985 he and Ron Bishop teamed up to make the TTU Crusaders a small college basketball powerhouse that posted 268 wins, 79 losses, and 4 NCCAA national championships. He was an old school Indiana Hoosier to his core with the intensity level of Bob Knight and an understanding of the intricacies of the game that was second to none.

The first day of TTU's team camp, Dad sat us all down in the hallway of the McGilvary gym and introduced Lefty.

"This is Coach Glascock and he's gonna be your coach for the week. He's here to make you better, so listen, play hard, and have fun."

It seemed like he was always reminding us to have fun, even though it was a tad unnecessary to remind this group. I'll never forget Lefty's first words to us.

"Do you guys like to guard?"

He could probably tell by the evil grins on our faces that we had bad intentions for our upcoming opponents.

"Yessir," we declared in unison.

"Well then, this should be a fun week, man," Lefty smirked.

Lefty often used the word 'man' as if it were a punctuation mark.

Our first game was against a JV team from North Carolina. These kids were all sophomores. They were huge and loomed over each one of us at the opening tip, seeming monstrous. A few of them even snickered at the little children they were about to play.

We played circles around these ogres. But the moment one of us would knife through the defense, we would run into a 16-year-old brick wall. A brick wall who would often, stuff the ball right back in our respective faces. Out of habit, we would run back on D, while Lefty paced up and down the sideline urging us to get up and bring the heat. It didn't come naturally to us at first.

Temple High had always been serious about defense. Dad's system at the high school had been dominated by stingy half court man-to-man defense and a post-oriented offense. Dad always coached to the strength of his personnel, and up to this point, the program at Temple High was known for strong inside play.

Our defensive principles were instilled into our brains at a young age. Sitting down in a stance, being on the help line, and getting through screens were second nature to even the middle schoolers. He was intentional about instilling consistency and continuity of program throughout the entire school. Every coach in the program from 4th grade to JV was a Coach T convert, preaching the gospel of half court man-to-man defense to their congregation. To Dad, there was one way to win— the other team doesn't score.

But Dad was always looking to grow as a coach. He was trying to bring Lefty into the fold for his own growth as well as ours. Soon, his personnel would be the polar opposite of what he'd been coaching for the last 5 years. We were little, mean, and fast, and he was hell bent on putting us in a position to achieve greatness.

We played our hearts out, but they were just too big. We would play again in one hour. During that hour of down time, Lefty sat in a chair in the coffin corner of the gym. The seven of us sat Indian-style around him like kindergarten kids being read to by their teacher before nap time.

"Guys, I want you to tell me what happened out there," he said.

He then proceeded to ask us question after question.

"What happened when you guys drove to the basket?" he asked.

"We got swatted," Gabe said.

"What could you do to avoid that, Gabe?" Lefty prodded.

Gabe looked at the floor deep in thought for a few seconds.

"We could dish it to an open man."

"Well there ya go, Gabe." Lefty then went into situational detail about drawing the attention of help defenders by driving and finding open teammates.

Lefty shot the next question at us. "Okay. What else was tough for you?"

"Getting rebounds," Ricky said, without hesitation.

"Yep, doesn't take a rocket surgeon to see that was an issue, man."

We all chuckled.

Lefty continued, "If they get shots, we have to get rebounds. What if we didn't need to get so many rebounds, because they didn't get as many shots?"

It was like a light switch flipped on in our collective head.

He continued, "Look at you, man. Look at them. You ain't big. Odds are you never will be. But, you do have speed, you're all mean, and you can sit down in a stance and guard. For the rest of the week, let's get up and dog these kids. Whether we make or miss a shot, they don't get an inch of that court without having to fight us for it. We'll contest every pass they make. But don't just reach and try to take the ball away from your man. That'll get you fouls. Just be there, and we'll slowly break 'em by being relentless."

There were games being played on the courts, so he took us outside to the parking lot to teach the fine art of breaking the will of our opponents for the next half hour. He showed us how to take good angles when guarding the ball. How to apply effective pressure that did not rely on reaching to steal the ball from our man. He also showed us the proper positioning off the ball that would allow us to challenge passing lanes. It was nearly 100 degrees outside and Lefty was in a full sweat. It was time to go back in the gym and play again.

"We ain't gonna man handle them. We're gonna just be there. Always there. They'll get tired, we'll keep coming. They'll need a breather, but we'll never stop. Eventually, they won't even want the ball, man. When that starts to happen, we broke 'em. Just remember, they gotta fight us for every inch of the floor," Lefty reminded us as he led our small platoon back into the building.

This style would be perfect for our group. We could run for days. We could live in a low defensive stance, and would take a charge on a moving truck. The idea of breaking our opponent's will was right up our Highland Park alley. I never thought it possible, but basketball was about to get a lot more fun.

The next game, we faced a team from Alabama that was just as ogre-ish as the team we faced before. They snickered at us too. Gabe and I smirked as we made eye contact, then simultaneously glanced at Lefty. He looked angry (we figured out later that was just how he always looked) and mouthed the words, "Break 'em." And that is exactly what we did.

With Lefty's guidance, our young group was starting to develop an identity. It looked like Dad's plan to get the Left Hander involved had worked too. After coaching us for a few weeks, Lefty would become Dad's unofficial assistant coach.

Lefty Glascock in college

15

7TH GRADE WAS A new world for me and my class. At Temple, elementary school graduation was at the end of the 6th grade year, and 7th grade meant the first year of middle school at the big building that housed all the middle school and high school students. I would be walking the halls with my heroes, Andy, Karl, Nick, and Deas & Co. (the talented freshmen). This new adventure was exciting and nerve wracking at the same time. From day one, I wanted to make a good impression on my older peers, but I had a few things working against me.

After 'the Coog's' passing, Dad inherited a 1980 Toyota Corolla that his brother had left to him before he went back to the mission field in Peru. Dad called this rusty piece of work 'the Beast.' In the world of nasty cars, 'the Beast' had no rivals. It had over 300 thousand miles. The radio would randomly turn off and on if you hit any bumps in the road, and the volume level was unpredictable when this would occur. Dad would be driving along deep in thought or conversation; hit a pot hole, and have to slam his fist on the dash to get *Achy Breaky Heart* to stop blowing our eardrums. From the backseat, there was a hole in the interior where you could see the wheel spinning on the pavement. My sister and I would use this as our own personal trash can. The car's best feature was the driver's side door. It wouldn't latch, so the driver, or whoever was sitting behind the driver's seat (which was always me since I was the oldest), would have to reach their hand out the window and hold the door closed on right turns. During the cold months, I would don my Michael Jackson-esque one glove to hold the door. It was always an adventure, especially when we were running late to school. Dad would whip around the corner as we were approaching campus, trying to make it in before the bell. The door would often give my hand the slip as it flew open. Dad would reach out to grab the open door, while yelling at me in the backseat. He would naturally drift while closing it. Then he would over correct and hit a pot hole, and we would approach the school like a mobile Billy Ray Cyrus concert on the mean streets of Highland Park. It had to be a sight to see.

In the mornings I was always looking at the clock. I did whatever I could to make us get there as early as possible, so fewer of my peers in the courtyard would see and hear 'the Beast' creeping into the lot. If we were on time, I went to my delay game, the four corners. Every bite of my Cinnamon Toast Crunch would be deliberate and savored. I would read every word on the back of the box and all the nutrition facts on the side that I didn't even understand, before I finished my bowl. It was worth getting honked at and yelled at by Dad for being slow to get to the car. I had to make sure we got to school either early or late, because there was no greater embarrassment for this 7th grade poser than 'the Beast.'

Before school started, Mom had taken us to Goody's to get some new clothes. In true 90's style, I got some Ivy Crew and Bugle Boy shirts, as well as some new jeans. I was gonna be lookin' fly on my first day of Jr. High. The first day of school, I had on my favorite new Bugle Boy shirt. I strutted down the hallway with a faux-confidence that could inspire posers for generations to come, arrived at my bottom locker and guess who had the top locker directly over me. That's right... Danny Deas. Deas was the 9th grade alpha and he was more than willing to welcome me to the new building.

"Well, look who it is," he said.

"What's up, Deas."

He looked at my shirt and pointed to the insignia on my right chest.

"Bugle Boy," he said, with his finger digging into my chest.

"Bugle man," he said, as he pointed to himself. He smiled and walked away.

Welcome to the big house, Josh. When I got home from school, I gave Mom all my Bugle Boy shirts to take back to Goody's, and said, "Mom, don't buy me any more Bugle Boy shirts."

Junior High is a weird stage in life.

16

THE ANTICIPATION FOR THE 1993-94 season was palpable for folks around Temple High. Andy and Karl were seniors, and Nick and Chambers were poised to perform on the big stage. This was the year everyone had been waiting for.

Gabe and I were lighting it up during my 7th grade season. He was a man amongst boys, dominating games with his physical presence alone, and I picked up exactly where I left off in elementary school, consistently knocking down the three ball. Halfway through the season, I started feeling a sharp pain on the inside of my right foot below the ankle. I played through it, but the pain would get worse with every practice and game. One day, Dad checked me out of school to go to the doctor. The x-rays showed a piece of bone had chipped off of the inside of my foot and had begun tearing through the tendon in my ankle. The doctor told us I would need surgery, but wouldn't do more damage by playing the rest of the season. It would just be painful. I was happy to hear that. He gave me a small donut shaped pad to put on the inside of my shoe to keep my shoe from irritating the injury.

We made it to the Jr. High championship game vs. District 4A rival Chattanooga Christian School. They had a good group of 8th grade players led by long, talented point guard Phil Jacobs. The game was close, but their size and depth would prove too much for us to overcome.

The day after the bitter conclusion of my 7th grade year, Temple High would host their biggest regular season game in school history. Perennial national powerhouse St. Anthony Friars from Jersey City, New Jersey would come to town to play us. They were coached by the legendary Bob Hurley. The Friars were ranked in the Top 5 in USA Today's high school basketball poll. Dad had called Coach Hurley the summer before and asked them to come down to Tennessee. Dad figured having such a nationally recognized program like St. Anthony in our gym would be a great fund raiser for our school and our program. He knew we probably wouldn't have a chance to beat them, but it would be a great experience for our guys as well as our city. I imagine getting games scheduled was not an easy task for Coach Hurley, because he quickly agreed to bring his team down to Chattanooga. When Dad had asked Coach Hurley how they were going to be that year, Coach Hurley replied, "Honestly coach, it's gonna be tough to make a pass against this group."

The event had taken the city by storm. Everyone wanted to see if the local little guy could hold its own with the best the country had to offer. The game would be played across the street in TTU's McGilvary Gym, because our home court at Vance couldn't handle a crowd of this magnitude. The preliminary bout put local powers McCallie and Howard High against each other in what was sure to be an instant classic. McCallie was a boarding school that looked like a college campus. It was white collar to the max. Their notable alumni included the likes of CNN founder Ted Turner and U.S. Congressman Zach Wamp. Led by Navy signee Ryan Lookabill, McCallie was the Princeton of Tennessee high school basketball. Howard High was at the opposite end of the basketball spectrum, a high octane, high flying juggernaut. Their game of high level yet contrasting styles combined with the real life David vs. Goliath event that would follow, would make for an unforgettable night of basketball in the city of Chattanooga. Two hours before the tip off of the McCallie/

Howard game, the ticket line was wrapping around the McGilvary Gym. This event was huge. The McCallie/ Howard game lived up to the hype, and was decided by a Ryan Lookabill 3 in the waning seconds.

The 2,500 seat gym was completely full during warm-ups for the main event. We raced off to a fast start by pounding it inside to Andy. The crowd was electric, but the Friars would not be rattled. They played full court man to man defense. It was the grown man version of the defense Lefty introduced to us at camp. During the first half, they rotated 5 different guys on Nick. Nick had to earn every inch of the floor vs. one jet fast, Division 1 caliber on-the-ball defender after another, for the entire first half. The substitution horn would go off every two minutes or so. A fresh, new jackrabbit would enter the game exchanging a high five with the one that had been dogging Nick up and down the floor during the previous two minutes. It was his turn to take a shot at breaking Nick. Nick was holding his own and we were doing a good job taking care of the ball and controlling the tempo. The halftime buzzer sounded, and we entered the locker room down by 5 points.

Dad couldn't help but think to himself, *This is happening. We could shock the country. All we have to do is keep it close. If it is a one or two possession game inside of two minutes, anything could happen.*

He entered the locker room and began sharing his thoughts with the team. He reviewed the game plan and made some adjustments. He closed his halftime speech with motivation.

"Guys you are 16 minutes away from taking down the giant. Just run the stuff, play together, and stay poised. You have the chance to do something that will never be forgotten in this city. Nobody has to be a hero. All we have to do is do what we do for two quarters. Let's go out their together and play the hardest 16 minutes of basketball we have ever played."

Our locker room sounded like a Holy Ghost revival at a Pentecostal church. Every player was jacked beyond belief as they noisily bounced up and down exiting the locker room. Everyone except Nick. Nick was still sitting inside a wooden locker with his mouth wide open, blankly staring at the spot where Dad was previously standing. Dad's assistant Terry Evans got his attention as he was about to walk out the door and pointed toward Nick. Dad walked over to talk to him.

"Are you okay, Nick?"

"Yeah, Coach. I just need a second," he sighed.

"What's the problem?" Dad asked

"Just tired, I'll be okay though. Just need some

water… and to sit here for a few more seconds," Nick said.

"Alright Nick, you can do this. During the game just let me know when you need a breather and Chambers will be ready to give you one," Dad said, trying to encourage him.

"I will coach," Nick said.

As Dad walked out the door, Nick said, "Coach…"

"Ya, Nick?"

"They're really fast," Nick said, with a nervous grin on his face.

"Yes, they are, Nick."

As Dad and Coach Evans walked out the tunnel back to the floor, Dad turned to Coach Evans.

"Terry, we're screwed."

Coach Evans erupted with laughter.

Nick Shiraef shooting a floater vs. St. Anthony's

Halfway through the third quarter, Nick walked over to the bench while a St. Anthony player shot a free throw.

"Coach, I can't go anymore. I just need a few minute break," he said.

Dad looked down the bench and hollered, "Chambers! Get Nick."

Chambers hopped up and sprinted to the scorer's table to check in. Running to the table at the same time from the Friar's bench was 5'5" freshman, Bernard Barrow. After high school, Barrow went on to be the starting point guard at George Washington University. Chambers played like a maniac. He was tough as nails and only knew one speed—full throttle. St. Anthony's made the free throw, triggering the substitution horn. When the ball was put in play, Chambers made a sharp cut to get open. Barrow was on his hip and forced him all the way to the baseline to get the ball. Chambers got the ball and took off like a bat out of hell to his right. Barrow effortlessly slid to cut him off and sent him back left. Chambers crossed over and went as hard left as he could. Barrow cut him off again. Chambers went back right. Barrow turned him again. Chambers sprint dribbled back left. Again, Barrow was there. As Chambers changed direction to try to get by him one more time, the whistle blew.

"Ten seconds!" the ref shouted, holding up both hands.

Chambers picked up the ball and looked down at his feet. Not only did he fail to get the ball across half court, he was still a good step inside the 3-point arc! He just looked at Dad with his palms in the air like he was thinking, *What am I supposed to do about this guy?*

St. Anthony's had broken our point guards and went on to win by 24 points. We played our guts out though, especially Nick. Come to find out later, Nick wasn't the only player who had been broken by St. Anthony's full court heat. On two different occasions earlier in the year, the opposing point guard had to make a post-game trip to the hospital to receive I.V. treatment for exhaustion and dehydration after facing the Friar's committee of will breakers. All five members of this nasty committee would go on to be Division 1 point guards.

After the game, Dad and Coach Dan Wadley (our athletic director and girls' basketball coach) took Bob Hurley and the Friars out to eat at Ryan's steakhouse. The coaches sat around a table and talked for hours as the players threw down epic portions of food. It looked like these guys hadn't eaten in months. I listened to them share stories and talk about how pretty the grass and trees were on our campus. Remember, our campus was in the middle of Highland Park. Grass and trees were actually pretty scarce, and the campus was downright nasty. I guess not to guys from Jersey City, they were another level of hard. As I listened, I found myself a little more grateful for the grass we had.

As we were leaving the restaurant, Coach Hurley turned to Dad and asked if they could practice in Vance at 6:30am before their flight left. Dad obliged.

The next morning, it was still dark when "the Beast" rolled up to the gym. I got up some shots while Dad rolled out the ball rack and set up the gym for practice. The Friars came rolling in around 6:15am and started to put on their gear while Dad talked with Coach Hurley and his staff.

St. Anthony Freshman point guard Bernard Barrow had sprained his ankle toward the end of our game the night before and came in hobbling on crutches. He would sit on a folding chair with his swollen foot immersed in a bucket of ice for the duration of the practice. Literally... the duration.

I swept the floor while the Friars laced 'em up and the coaches game-planned.

Coach Hurley surveyed the gym and said to his assistant coach, George Canda, "George, with Bernard out we need one more guard to give us our 3 teams of 5. Where do you think we could find another guard?"

Dad smiled.

"I don't know coach," Coach George smirked.

"Josh!" Coach Hurley yelled across the gym.

I stopped dead in my tracks and looked at Coach Hurley.

"Lace 'em up. We need you to practice today."

I ran to the bleachers to exchange my flip flops for my game shoes, (I was always prepared for a game to break out). As I was lacing 'em up my heart felt like it was beating twice as fast and about to burst through my chest, as I was equal parts excited and scared to death.

Practice began with a warm up that included the most challenging full court two ball dribbling drills I had ever attempted. The Friars made it look so easy while I kicked the balls all over the court. I spent more time chasing balls than I did dribbling. I ran through some other drills with them and it was all I could do to keep up.

They were like a well-oiled machine. Their passes were crisp. Their cuts were sharp. Their cohesiveness was spell binding as they moved together like an amoeba at both ends. The players reverence for Coach Hurley was awesome. When he spoke, you could hear a pin drop. Each player stood motionless at attention with their eyes transfixed on him. He coached them hard and was incapable of sugar coating anything, because brutal honesty was his M.O. The standard of excellence he held his players to while they were on the floor, was higher than anything I had seen in my young life.

Dad learned a great deal from Coach Hurley and St. Anthony's. There were many takeaways that would come in handy for our varsity team later that year, and for years to come. For me, it was inspiring to see the defensive philosophy that Lefty had been preaching to us executed to perfection at the highest level of high school basketball, and I wanted to be just like them.

17

B Y TOURNAMENT TIME THE 1993-94 Varsity Crusaders were playing their best ball of the season. Andy was having an All-State year and the team was clicking on all cylinders. District 4A was loaded with talent. Temple, Lookout Valley High, Boyd Buchanan School, and Chattanooga Christian had set themselves apart as 'The Big 4' of the league. We had been swept by CCS, had swept Boyd, and had split with Lookout Valley during the regular season. We would face Lookout Valley in the District Semifinals. We came out guns blazing and pounding the ball inside as we advanced to the finals.

In the District 4A championship we would face off against the guard oriented Chargers from Chattanooga Christian. Savvy, sharpshooting point guard Wes Moore was their man. After high school, Wes Moore would walk on at University of Tennessee at Chattanooga his freshman year in college. He played so well that he earned a scholarship going into his sophomore year. His senior year at Chattanooga, he led the Mocs to their first and only NCAA tournament Sweet 16, while becoming the university's all-time leader in assists and steals. His backcourt mate at CCS was Jimmy Whitaker, a lights-out 3-point bomber.

It is difficult to beat a good team three times, and our team had gotten much better since our last game vs. CCS. Dad took a loaner under the arm from the Bob Hurley playbook. We were going to 'St. Anthony' Wes Moore. He had already proven that he couldn't be guarded by one player, so we would dog him by committee. We picked him up full court and rotated five guys on Wes in the first half. Half way through the second quarter, it was starting to take a toll on him. He started to get rid of the ball early instead of knifing through the teeth of our defense to create shots for himself and Whitaker. Since Whitaker always leeched off of Wes's ability to draw a crowd, he couldn't get off any clean looks. We went into the half with a 9-point lead. The plan was working to perfection, but Dad wouldn't be satisfied until we broke him.

When the teams took the floor to warm up for the second half, Dad looked toward the other end and didn't see Wes in the layup line with the rest of the team. As his eyes surveyed the floor, he could not believe what he saw. Wes was sitting on the baseline beside the water cooler with his feet straight out in front of him leaning back on his hands. One of the gumbies from the end of their bench was standing directly in front of him waving a towel like a fan to cool him off. Dad nudged Mark Chambers (our hardest guard who had won the draw to be Wes's primary defender).

"Hey Chambers..." Dad said with a smirk. "Check this out." He glanced in the direction of Wes, who looked like an Egyptian pharaoh being fanned by a Hebrew slave.

A sinister grin appeared on Chambers face. Not only could he smell the blood in the water, he could see it with his own eyes.

"He's broke, Coach. We got him."

Chambers made his rounds to the other mad dogs in our Wes-dogging committee. They would each glance toward the other end and smile with a sense of satisfaction, and a hunger for more blood.

He did break. His shots were short, and he was too fatigued to break our defense down like he had done to us and every other team he had faced during his career.

We ended up winning the game by twenty points,

and would carry that momentum into region tournament play.

The tournament setup in Tennessee is strange. Districts are comprised of 8-10 teams. Regions are comprised of 2 districts. The top 4 finishers in a district tournament advance to an 8 team region tournament. The 2 teams that make it to the region championship advance to the sub-state. The winner gets to host the runner up from the neighboring region. The loser has to go on the road to play in a hostile environment. The sub-state is a one game showdown to see who advances to the state tournament. It's crazy because you can actually lose three times in post season play but still make it to the state tournament. The overall strength of District 4A was rare. Usually, the 8 best teams in the Region were in District 4A, yet only 4 would advance to the region tournament. District play was murderer's row, year after year. Every year, one of the strongest teams in the entire state would get bounced in the region semifinals, by an equally strong District 4A rival. This was the game that everyone looked forward to as do or die. One gym, one night, four heated rivals playing for their tournament lives. It was the most pressure packed night of the year. After winning our respective first-round games, we faced Boyd in the region semis. Boyd had young talent that would go on to do great things, but this was the year of the Crusader. Andy and Karl would not be denied.

Temple/CCS round 4 was upon us. We had the momentum and mental edge due the district championship rout the week before. Watching the game was like Déjà vu. Same story, one week later. Our 5-man mad-dog committee harassed Wes up and down the floor. We went on to win in convincing fashion, again claiming the Region 2A crown.

Karl Lewis knocks down a jumper in the Vance Gym

18

DAD'S TEAM WOULD BE hosting Oneida High School in the sub-state. Oneida was a school that had a strong basketball tradition from outside of Knoxville. They were easily the best team in our neighboring region, but they were upset in their region championship. So they had to hit the road. They were led by All-State performer and scoring machine, 6'2" guard, Troy Yaden, and 6'10" Wake Forest signee Rodney Dale West. West hadn't played in any tournament games because of a bout with mononucleosis, and he was not expected to play against us either.

Our team was ready. We could taste a state berth. When the teams took the floor to warm up, West was the last player in the layup line decked out in full gear with a flak jacket under his jersey that made him look 4 months pregnant. It looked like he would be playing after all. This game was destined to be a no-holds barred street fight to the finish, and it didn't disappoint.

It was close the entire way. The score was tied with seconds remaining when Yaden drove the lane with Chambers riding his hip, and let go a floater that just made it over Andy's outstretched shot blocking right hand. Karl stepped in front of West to block out his attempt at an offensive rebound. The ball caromed high off the rim. Karl and West jumped for the ball at the same time. West, being 5 inches taller than Karl, reached straight up and grabbed the ball as it was making its descent. He landed and jumped straight backwards away from Karl with his arms still extended from the rebound, and let go a fade away, high release shot a fraction of a second before the horn sounded. Splash. Heartbreak.

Rodney Dale was mobbed by his teammates as Karl collapsed to the floor. West was a head taller than all his teammates. Their bouncing bundle of celebratory glee bounced closer and closer to the dejected Temple student section. West proceeded to take off his jersey and waive it above his head while yelling at our stunned student body from the middle of this cluster of humanity. He then threw his jersey into our crowd. It was snatched by one of our rowdy students who proceeded to lunge forward over the top of two rows of fans in his attempt to throw it right back in his face. Coach Wadley and our principal Dr. Clayton Hunt knew emotions were running high, so they rushed over to pro-actively stand in front of our students to keep any potential hot heads from coming out of the stands and doing something stupid. It could've gotten real ugly fast. The guys pulled themselves together for a moment and lined up to shake hands with the victors with their heads held high.

I always learned a lot watching the older guys compete. This group was Temple warrior culture at its very best. They set the example for young players and teams in the program to follow. Their practice habits, their level of compete, their unselfishness, and their love for each other and their coaches was nothing short of inspiring. I thought I knew a little something about passion for competing with a team of brothers, but nothing had prepared me for what my young eyes would witness in the locker room that night.

I snuck in the door and played witness to a moment of purity in high school basketball. Andy was sitting on the first row of benches in front of the dry erase board sobbing into his jersey. Most of the guys were sitting in their lockers slumped over staring at the floor in a state of shock. Freshman Danny Deas and Jeremy Kennedy were sitting straight up in their lockers with tears welling up in their eyes observing the emotional display of the seniors. Dad and Coach Evans were standing in the corner waiting on Karl who had not come in yet. I don't know what he was doing out there. My guess is he just didn't want to leave the floor yet.

Karl had a high and tight crew cut and was built like a house. He just looked mean all the time. It wasn't just looks either. He was one of the baddest dudes Dad ever coached. He walked in with his head down and walked directly toward Dad.

He said, "I'm sorry, Coach," as he buried his face in Dad's right clavicle and broke down.

Dad said, "No Karl," and held him while they both cried for what seemed like five minutes.

He kept repeating, "I'm so sorry. I tried. I'm just so sorry."

Dad tried to console him, saying, "Karl, you did all you could do. I'm so proud of you. There is nothing to be sorry about."

When Karl finally let go, he and Andy went around the room and hugged the neck of every one of their teammates, apologizing for not getting them to Murfreesboro. He approached Deas and Jeremy, and told them to enjoy it because it would be over before they knew it.

I stood in a dark corner and squalled. I could hardly breathe. Their passion for the game inspired me. At this moment, I also realized the mortality of a basketball career was inevitable, no matter how good you were. All careers must die. Pain will come with it. But if your career must die, make it a warrior's death with your brothers at arms. This was high school basketball done right. This was why Dad coached. Leave it on the floor together. Love each other. Share the victories as well as the heartbreaks, in pursuit of something bigger than any one person.

That night, I laid in my bed with the lights out and my eyes wide open. After about an hour rolling around in a sleepless frustration, I turned on the lamp beside my bed, grabbed my notebook, and wrote about what I had seen. The last sentence I wrote was: *The high school guys really love Dad... and Temple basketball.*

19

A FTER THE SEASON, I had surgery on my foot to remove the bone fragment and was laid up for six weeks. Dad had been trying to get me to take a break for a while now. He wasn't happy I had to have surgery, but he was glad that I would be resting my body. I hated being on crutches and didn't know what to do with myself. Depression started to set in—not the hopeless kind of depression, but the bored kind that sets in when a young active boy is forced to become a hobbling old codger for 6 weeks. But there was a light in the midst of the nearly unbearable boredom. That light was March Madness—my favorite time of the year.

Dad and I shared a love for the game, so naturally, we shared a love for March Madness and the NBA Playoffs as well. Every night the rays seeped into our brains as we consumed and digested each play. I listened to Dad pick apart and coach up the best players in the country, slowly fortifying my knowledge of the game and cementing our relationship.

I would ask questions constantly. "Dad, why did Dean Smith go to a zone there? Man D is the best and UNC's man is so good."

"Because Rasheed Wallace just got his 3rd foul and Dean wants to keep him on the floor. He is trying to protect him from getting his 4th."

He would ask me questions, "Josh, what do you think Jeff McInnis could do to speed up the tempo of this game?"

"Pitch it ahead with a pass more?"

"Yes, he could definitely do that," Dad would say as he proceeded to give me more options. "What about the team getting more stops? Rebounds are easier to run on than pulling the ball out of the net. What about sprinting the ball up the floor to put pressure on Wake's transition D instead of walking it up? What about talking to his teammates during dead ball time? Encouraging them to run harder. Or telling the throw-in man to get the ball out of the net and get it to him quicker on made shots."

These entertaining, yet learning moments would occur on a near nightly basis. I learned as much basketball while we watched college games on TV as I did during my entire playing experience. He was coaching me without me even realizing he was coaching me. I was just having a great time watching the games with my Dad.

Now I realize that his indirect coaching was molding and shaping my young basketball mind. It was his secret weapon. If he had relied strictly on coaching and critiquing my play on the court during my formative years, we probably would have wanted to kill each other by my sophomore year in high school. Instead, Dad was my best friend, and my fire for the game was constantly burning.

After the six weeks, I had made a full recovery and was ready to get back onto the floor to work on my game. We now had a tradition of Sunday and Wednesday night open gym at Vance. Word was getting out around town that we had the best open gym. Part of that was due to the way Dad ran the open gyms—no whining and defense called fouls. You respected the game or you were not allowed in the doors. It was his gym, so everyone that played had to play by his rules. The games were played by 2's and 3's to 15. Winner holds the court. Dad split the gym into two courts. He made sure that the best players played on one floor and everyone else played on the other floor. Of course, guys would get mad, but if they didn't like it, they could leave. It was the most competitive and efficient open gym in the city. Many of the best players in Chattanooga—past and present—played pick up in Vance on Sunday and Wednesday nights. This summer, I would graduate to the big boy court.

I would make my regular stops at the two team camps at TTU and Don Meyer's camp at Lipscomb, and even added a few more quality stops on my summer basketball camp tour. The first of which was Bob Hurley basketball camp in Rhode Island. In April, Coach Hurley gave Dad a call and invited us and a few of my teammates to Rhode Island to spend a week with him at camp. It was a 'thank you' for Dad's hospitality to the Friars when they came to our place. All we had to pay for was our plane tickets. Dad was in. He viewed spending a week with Coach Hurley as the best professional development move he could make. The last week in June, we—Dad, Gabe, Gabe's older brother A.J., and I— arrived in Portsmouth, Rhode Island, ready to get better.

Dad spent his days with Coach Hurley, teaching basketball all day. Gabe, A.J., and I worked on our games doing station drills led by coaches from all over New England, and competing with high caliber players in our age group. It was a great week. The highlight of the week was watching one of my childhood point guard heroes Bobby Hurley work out during the camp's after-hours. Bobby had been in a motorcycle accident that nearly claimed his life the year before. He was trying to get his body and game in shape for an NBA comeback. I thought Darin went hard in work outs. This guy was on another level. He worked out at a blinding speed that would make any game look like a cake walk. Gabe, A.J., and I were watching him in awe when Dad snuck in behind us and put his hand on my shoulder.

"Guys, when your workouts look like that, the games become slow and easy," he said.

Brilliant. As we watched the rest of his workout, I scribbled each drill into my notebook. If it was good enough for Bobby Hurley, surely this workout could do wonders for my game.

20

THE NEXT STOP ON my summer basketball camp tour before my 8th grade year would be Point Guard College run by basketball author and former Duke point guard Dick Devenzio. Point Guard College was expensive. It was $400 for four days of intense basketball. Dad came up with a plan for me to earn some money to go to the camp. He never just gave me anything. If I wanted something or wanted to attend a camp, he came up with a plan for me to earn it with some good old fashioned hard work. It was usually in the form of landscaping projects in the massive sloped yard of our new house.

The first one was brutal. He wanted to build a retaining wall with volleyball sized rocks at the bottom of the hill in the back yard. He paid me $5 an hour to haul the rocks from the top of the driveway (where the dump truck had unloaded a massive pile) to the bottom of the hill where our retaining wall would be. We would then place them one by one to build the wall that would be about 6 feet high and 60 feet long. It was hard work, but I felt a great sense of accomplishment.

The slogan for this camp was "Think the Game." The brochure featured a picture of Auguste Rodin's sculpture, *The Thinker,* with a basketball superimposed on its head. This was right up my alley. Dad had read Dick's book called *Stuff, Good Players Should Know.* It was his basketball Bible. Each chapter was short and to the point, so you could read it in short sittings. Dick must have been aware that most athletes have a very short attention span. The concepts in this book were genius in their simplicity and practicality. Dick thought outside the box and had a way of saying things that you would not forget. He used made-up words like 'P-dribble,' 'SOFO,' and 'SCHAPE,' to get his points stuck in your head. I had begun reading the book on the drive and was blown away with his thought processes. Dad had done his research. He was feeling pretty confident about the new basketball expert in whose hands he would place my development for the week.

As we arrived at camp, Dad reminded me to fill up my notebook and maximize the short week. He wanted to make sure I was focused, because this was a hefty investment for a family with our income level.

The camp was for players from 8th grade to college. It just so happened that I was the only 8th grader there. It was for serious players only, and Dick wouldn't cater to clowns. He didn't care if you had a good time or not. He did this to help players get better. Despite being the youngest player there, I was intent on getting the most out of the week.

We dropped off my gear in my room for the week and met Reggie, my new roommate. Reggie was a big, strong sophomore in high school from South Carolina who had a tattoo of a tiger on his left shoulder. Not many 16-year-olds had tattoos in 1995. Despite his intimidating look, Reggie was a really nice kid.

When registration had concluded, Dick's brother Dave met with the parents in the gym to explain what we would be doing during the week, while Dick walked us to a classroom in the building next door. We filed into the room and made our way to our desks as Dick walked to the front, sat on a stool, and waited for us to be seated. I sat up in my desk with my pen ready to scribble down every word that came out of Dick's mouth.

Dick opened the week with an unforgettable monologue introduction that would cover who he was, who Point Guard College was for, and how we could get the most out of the week. His opening words are etched in my memory.

"Welcome to Point Guard College. I hope you are ready to 'think the game.' You are here to get better. You are not here to have fun. If you just want to have fun, you are probably at the wrong place, but I ain't gonna be mad at ya. Just don't keep anyone else from maximizing their week and we'll be fine," he said. He then proceeded to tell us the schedule for the week.

"...This is Point Guard COLLEGE. You will be treated as college athletes. Class will begin at 8:30am every morning. If you are tired, and you don't want to come to class, you don't have to. Look, I have your money. It won't bother me one bit. If you aren't serious about learning more about the game, you won't hurt my feelings. Just don't get in anyone else's way."

Before we dove head first into his plethora of basketball wisdom, he gave us the rules for the week.

"Okay, I only have a few rules. Since you are college athletes this week, I will expect you to respect our championship environment. So, I don't really feel the need to give a bunch of rules. Guys stay off the girl's floor. If you are caught on the girl's floor you will be sent home."

"Respect the facilities. The university was kind enough to let us use their facilities this week. So have some maturity and don't mess anything up. Just like at a store, if you break it, you buy it."

Look, I was from a small Christian school. We had rules for everything under the sun. Rules for clothing. Rules for relationships. Rules for music and movies. Rules for lifestyle. If you could think it, the school had a set of rules for it. I thought that was completely normal. It was all I knew. This place was a different world. Coming from my background, Dick's final rule absolutely blew my mind...

"Curfew is at 11:30—lights out and time to get rested for the next day. I'm not going to walk the halls and check to make sure all the kiddies are in bed. You are college athletes this week, and you will need your rest. If you don't wanna go to bed, just don't keep anyone up who is serious about getting better. And dammit, if you are sneaking around somewhere after curfew, and you see me... nod. I'll nod back and we'll go our separate ways, because I'm probably sneaking somewhere too. Point Guards have to be sneaky."

The class erupted with laughter. I thought to myself, "This is going to be the best week of my life."

I filled up 10 pages of notes during the first class-room session. I wrote down everything (even the curse words). I had even written down 'Point Guards have to be sneaky' at the top of the first page and underlined it twice.

On our walk from the classroom to the gym I started looking around at all the players. Everyone was taller than me, even the girls. It shouldn't have bothered me because I was used to playing with older and bigger guys, but I was a little intimidated at first. Everyone here was probably just as serious about playing ball as I was. I was the youngest and the smallest. I couldn't help but think... *I hope I'm not the worst player here.*

When we got in the gym for the first session, Dick left it up to the players to organize themselves into 3 even lines at the 6 baskets. I put on my game shoes and stood near a corner looking for a friendly basket to join. Preferably, one that didn't have too many big mean looking guys, and did have a pretty girl or two.

Reggie saw me looking over the gym and shouted toward me from one of the goals on the main court. "Hey Josh, come hoop with us."

He didn't have to tell me twice, and I hustled over to his basket. Reggie was a good player and physically imposing for his age. He took it upon himself to be my older brother for the week. I don't know if he felt sorry for me because I looked so lost and nervous, or if he was just a guy who had younger siblings that he acted as protector for. Either way, I was glad he was there to help me loosen up.

The daily schedule was intense. Each day would consist of 3 classroom sessions that ranged from 45 minutes to 2 hours. Each classroom session would be followed by a 90+ minute court session where we would work on the concepts that Dick spoke about during his lecture.

The week went great. Dick was just like Dad in the way that he would coach players up. He would let players fail, then guide them to an understanding of what they could have done better. He would use the question method to get players to think the game for themselves, as opposed to spoon feeding the answers. I don't think Dick said more than 4 or 5 sentences to me on court all week. He coached the biggest and best players. He coached the alphas of the group to be leaders. Every gym session, I would receive solid coaching from Reggie and another high schooler at my goal named Brian. The format was as necessary as it was genius, because it was just Dick and Dave with 50 athletes. It was hands-on leadership training at its finest for the older kids. The rest of us were getting great coaching from our more experienced peers and taking in vast amounts of knowledge in the classroom.

I was walking back to the dorm on the last night

of camp with Reggie and a few other athletes when someone behind me called my name. I spun around. It was Dick! He motioned for me to come back and walk with him. I ran, anxious for the opportunity.

"Josh, great job this week. Watching you battle the bigger players was impressive. Keep working and you will have a bright future ahead of you," he said.

"Thanks, Coach. And thanks for teaching me so much this week. My notebook is almost full, "I said, as I proudly flashed my roughed up notebook.

"That's great. Keep reviewing those notes through-out your career. You never know when you might need a reminder," he said. "Josh, you're probably never go-ing to be big. So you'll have to make your living by being a better BASKETBALL PLAYER than everyone else. You're going to have to out think them as well as out work them. And you'll have to be crafty. After watching you this week, I believe you'll be just fine as long as you never stop pursuing knowledge, and never stop adding dimensions to your game."

"Yes sir. Thank you again," I said, with my chest puffed out with pride.

"You got it, buddy."

I ran up to join the rest of the group.

Dick hung out in the lobby of the dorm talking basketball and answering questions from all the athletes that were huddled around him. He was a true thinker of the game, enlightening us with each word that would slip from his lips. He stuck around for a little over two hours before he told us he was going to cash in for the night, and we all went our separate ways. Point Guard College with Dick Devenzio was hands-down the most enlightening, inspiring week of my basketball career.

After the conclusion of the final ceremony the next morning, Dad and I got in the car to head back to the house.

"How was it?" he asked.

"Awesome," I replied. "Can I go twice next year?"

PART 2

THE COACH'S SON

21

JR. HIGH PRACTICE HAD begun. My foot was one-hundred percent, and I was playing the best basketball of my young life. I had improved more over this last summer than I had in any summer before. Dad was sitting in his office during the last period of the day when there was a knock at the door. Mike Erhart (my new Jr. High coach) peeked in and said, "Coach, can we talk for a minute?"

"Sure Mike. Come on in," Dad replied.

Coach Erhart pulled up a chair and said, "Coach, I think you should consider moving Josh up to J.V."

"Ah man... is he being a jackwagon and giving you problems?" he asked, concerned that I was having attitude issues.

"Oh no. Nothing like that, Coach," Mike replied. "I just think it would be best for him. Even more, it'd be best for his teammates."

"I'm not sure," Dad said. "I really would like him to get to play with his classmates and learn from you. I'll also be coaching him for 4 years, and I don't know if he could handle five years of being the coach's son."

"I understand that," Mike said. "Just come watch practice tonight and you'll see what I'm talking about."

During our practice, Dad sat in the balcony and watched from above. We did a few drills followed by a long organized scrimmage. Coach Erhart wanted to be sure Dad got to see the full dynamic between me and my teammates.

After seeing the scrimmage, the decision was a no brainer for Dad. When one of my teammates would catch the ball or get a rebound, they wouldn't even look at the goal. They wouldn't look to dribble either. They would lock their eyes on me and wait until I came to relieve them of their ball possessing responsibilities. It was clear that I would be holding back their improvement. I wouldn't develop either because it would be a one-man show. I needed to play with others and continue to develop the non-shooting aspects of my game.

Dad and Coach Erhart talked after practice and made the decision for me to move up to J.V. Coach Erhart got it. He knew that Jr. High basketball was not about winning and losing games. It was about the development of the kids.

I was now officially playing for Dad.

I missed my boys on the Junior High team, especially my neighborhood running mate Joel. But I was excited to be playing for Dad and with Gabe again. Dad coached both the J.V. and Varsity teams so both teams would practice together every day. Lefty came to practice almost every day now too. Despite being in his 40's he would gear up and play most days, and his level of intensity was infectious. Dad would run us through our normal skill drills and work on offensive execution and special situations for the first 90 minutes of practice. Then, he would turn over the last 30 minutes to the Left Hander. Lefty was our maestro of defense, and Dad gave him carte blanche to put his expertise into action to help our team become one of the best defensive teams in the state of Tennessee. At first, the players dreaded Lefty time. It meant sitting in a stance for minutes at a time, zig zag drills, slow slides, team defense break downs, diving on the floor after loose balls, and taking charges. Yes... we actually practiced taking charges. Every day we closed practice with defense in our minds.

Most days after practice, a group of us would stick around and pick Dad's brain. We just loved listening to him talk about basketball. He was our basketball Socrates. Challenging us with daily questions and allowing our discussions to flow freely. His stories were what we enjoyed the most though.

About one week into practice, Dad, Gabe, Ricky, Braucht and I were engaged in a Socratic basketball discussion. We had been getting roughed up by the varsity crew and didn't like losing. As per usual, Dad asked questions to get us to think. He then gave us some pointers that would help us compete better against our bigger, more experienced opponents. While he was talking, he paused mid-sentence and looked out onto the floor and saw Lefty shooting by himself on the main basket.

He turned to me and said, "Josh, you wanna get better? Go play Lefty one on one."

I looked at Lefty, then looked at Dad, then back to Lefty and said, "He'll kill me."

Lefty could shoot and was mean as a rattlesnake. He was in incredible shape for a man in his forties. Come to think of it, he was in incredible shape for a man of any age.

Dad replied, "So what if he kills you. You're tired of losing to the older, bigger guys' right? Well, you're gonna be playing against older, bigger players for a while, so you might as well start with the biggest, baddest dog in the yard."

I knew he was right. I reluctantly walked toward Lefty and said, "Hey Coach. Wanna play one on one?"

"Sure, man," Lefty replied, as he threw me the ball. "We'll play to 20 by 2's and 3's. Make it, take it. You gotta guard to get the ball."

We checked it up.

I was wearing my Lipscomb basketball camp T-shirt that had a cartoon caricature team picture on the back. It had been signed by every player and Coach Meyer. I was so proud of that shirt, despite it having a stupid looking pocket on my right chest. I had the ball in a triple threat position at the top of the key and started to measure Lefty up. I jab stepped a few times to try to get him off balance. Before I could make my first move toward the goal, he took a bear-like swipe at the ball. I quickly moved the ball so he wouldn't knock it out of my hands. His claw whisked across my chest in a violent downward motion, ripping the pocket clean off of my prized t-shirt. I took a step back and looked down at my chest. The pocket was hanging upside down and you could see my chest through the new hole in my shirt. Blood started to come out of two fresh scratches to the left of my nipple and slowly trickle down to my belly.

Lefty stood up and said, "My bad, man. I'll buy you a new shirt. Now check it up."

I didn't want him to think I was scared, even though I was, but I was pissed too. That savage old man just wrecked my favorite shirt and almost took my nipple clean off. I tried to act hard, checked it up, and he proceeded to beat me every way possible for the next hour. After that day, we played one on one almost every day after practice. I just thought if I could beat him, I could beat anybody. I don't think I won a game the whole year.

22

THE 1994-95 SEASON WAS a disappointing one for the varsity. Andy and Karl had left big shoes to fill. Nick's back court mate, Mark Chambers was no longer with the program. On the last day of school the year before, Chambers thought it would be hilarious to go from classroom to classroom with a lit cigarette in his mouth to thank all of his teachers and wish them a good summer break. The school administration did not find it funny in the least. He was asked not to come back to school the next year. Deas & Co. were sophomores, but they were still green. Nick made a valiant effort to carry the team and had a great year statistically, but we were upset in the quarterfinals of the District 4A tournament by a talented South Pittsburg team. Despite Nick's effort, we finished the year 19-9, marking the first time Temple High had failed to reach twenty wins since Dad's first year at the helm.

Our JV team had a good year and got better every day, and I enjoyed my first year playing for Dad. He never put up with any nonsense, but he coached from the world of positivity. I'm not saying he never yelled at us, because that would be a lie. When his players let even the slightest bit of corruption into their athletic souls, he would often blow a gasket. If you wanted to play for Temple you had to bring 4 values to the table: you had to work hard, be coachable, embrace personal responsibility, and be a great teammate. He held each of his players accountable for these values every day. We never had a team meeting that stated our core values or who we were. It was understood because it was instilled consistently into every player that wore the Red and White, and our program grew stronger in our values each year because knowledge was passed down by the upperclassmen.

On one particular Monday practice, we were playing a pressing game and I couldn't get open against bigger, faster sophomore point guard Jeremy Kennedy. I danced back and forth trying to shake him, but he blanketed my every move. Dad stopped the action with a loud, "Ho!" He always used voice instead of a whistle because he wanted our ears to be trained to his voice during games. "Josh, you can't beat a guy faster than you speed for speed, so quit dancing around. Get contact, get him off balance, then break hard for the ball." He demonstrated the move as he spoke. When he went back to his folding chair on the baseline, the ball went back into play. I walked into Jeremy and tried to get open, but he held my jersey just enough to stay with me and keep me covered. Then I went right back to dancing to get open.

"Ho!" He kicked his chair backwards, causing it to crash into the bleachers and I had a split-second flashback of the folding chair flying through the air and making that same crashing noise when Darin took that cursed dunk attempt. Everyone froze, eyes locked on Dad.

"Josh, what did I just say?"

"But, he was holding me."

Everyone stood silent awaiting the showers of non-blessings that were about to rain down on me.

"There are no 'buts' in big boy basketball, Josh!" He screamed at the top of his lungs. "You always have an answer, don't you?"

This had been the piece of my character that had driven Dad crazy during my 14 years on the earth. I often had an answer for everything, an excuse for doing whatever I did. If I got in trouble at school, it was because the teacher wasn't teaching us anything and couldn't control the class, or the rule was stupid and made no sense. I didn't always get along with my teachers, principals, school deans, security guards on Temple's campus, and well, basically anyone in authority over me that wasn't teaching me nuances of the game or wasn't named Kevin Templeton. This kind of stuff got my hide tanned or got me grounded more often than anything else. Dad would never attach any weight to my well thought out, perfectly logical reasoning for acting like a 'jackwagon' (as he would so eloquently put it). He just knew that I was usually wrong, yet I always thought I was right. In the words of Charles Barkley, one of the great philosophers of our time, "Benefit of the doubt comes with past experience."

I had made a mistake that was a two-fold no-no with Dad. It was one that all the older players knew not to make and the youngins would learn from either experience or by witnessing the unfortunate experience of a teammate.

First, I made the same mistake twice, which meant I was either uncoachable in the moment, or I wasn't focused. Both of which were unacceptable to Dad.

Second, I had made an excuse, so I had to face a full measure of wrath from the greatest coach I knew. As he ripped into me, he was also making sure that our core values got reinforced to every player.

He was also big on role definition. Everyone's role was communicated clearly to them, and he made sure we each knew what we needed to work on if we wanted to expand our role on the team. He was an empowering coach, especially on the offensive end, because he celebrated players making plays within their roles. As long as it was good shot selection, he never got angry at anyone for missing a shot. During that year, my J.V. teammate Braucht Walters randomly started having a hard time making wide open layups. Braucht was only 5'7", but he was a good player and an even better athlete. For some strange reason, open layups were a thorn in his side for about a month. Braucht would smack himself on the head and mumble things under his breath each time he missed a bunny in practice. It was in his head.

It made me mad too, because I was always on his team, and we needed those missed layups. I was set on being a good teammate and kept encouraging him, but man, I wanted him to fix this layup problem because I wanted to win in practice. One day on the way home from practice, I said, "Dad, how come you never get mad at Braucht for missing wide open layups?"

"Josh, do you honestly think there is anyone in the gym that wants Braucht to make that layup more than Braucht."

He didn't say another word about it, and just left me to chew on it for a while. Dad knew Braucht was trying his best, so it didn't make any sense to get angry about it. Dad would give coaching if something was technically off, but that's it. His philosophy took a lot of pressure off of shooting the basketball and allowed us to play with a clear head and sense of freedom that gave each of us the best chance to play our fearless best.

23

NEAR THE END OF the season I started feeling a dull pain in my knee. It wasn't enough to keep me from playing, but it seemed to be getting worse every day. During our last JV game, I loaded up to jump for a layup and my left knee just gave out from under me. I went straight to the floor before I could even get off the ground. It wasn't even that painful. It just felt like it collapsed under me. I got up and walked it off. The move had looked very awkward and un-athletic so Dad took me out. He was sure I had gotten hurt, while I was adamant that I was fine and asked to go back in the game. He told me to go back in the corner and do some lateral slides to see how it felt. I slid to the right and cut back left. It felt fine. I slid to the left and planted my left foot to cut back right. It completely gave out again. I was done. Something was definitely wrong.

The next day Dad and I made another trip to the doctor, where they took X-rays. As we waited for the results, I was feeling pretty low. Thinking about the possibility of having to be on crutches again and missing the camp season made me feel ill. When the doctor came back in, he had a concerned look on his face. He placed the X-rays on the illuminator, pulled out his pen, and started telling us about the damage. I had developed a lesion in my knee due to the loss of cartilage from daily wear and tear. The loss of cartilage meant bone on bone contact. The condition was called Osteochondritis Dessecans. It would take micro-fracture surgery to fix the damage. I started to tear up as he told us that I would be on crutches for another six weeks.

Dad was concerned about my body. He would make sure that I didn't rush my recovery or put much stress on my body during this summer. I had my surgery and made a full recovery. My six week follow up appointment meant that I got to lose the crutches and start walking again. If I had it my way, I would've gotten out of the car and gone straight to Tripp's house to shoot, but Dad wasn't having any of that. When we got in the car, he explained to me how the summer would go.

"Josh, you are too young to be having surgeries," he said. "Especially surgeries due to the pounding you are putting on your body. You're gonna take it easy this summer"

"But, Dad—" he stopped me before I could explain to him that I would be fine.

"But... nothing. This is non-negotiable," he said. "Do you want to make varsity next year?"

"More than anything," I replied.

"Okay. Then you gotta do what I say. Your size is going to make it tough. You have to have your body. If you are not 100%, you won't be able to play," he said." You can shoot, but it has to be low impact. You won't be going to Lipscomb or Point Guard College. I'm not even sure about team camp. We gotta make sure this knee is taken care of. Do you understand?"

"Yessir," I said.

I wasn't happy, but I wanted to make varsity next year, so I would do whatever I had to do, even if that meant taking it easy this summer. I sat out every camp besides the last TTU team camp. Dad helped me make a low impact shooting workout. By July, my knee was 100%, but Dad made sure I wouldn't be pounding my knee too much by putting me to work every day on a new outdoor project.

24

THE 1995-96 BASKETBALL SEASON was underway. I was 5'6" 110-pound freshman and made the varsity team. We only had one senior, Nathan Templeton, my cousin. He had been living in Peru for the last 10 years. His parents were missionaries and they wanted to send him back to the states for his senior year of high school. Mom and Dad took him in to live with us. We now had eight people living in our four-bedroom house in Georgia, and I had a new roommate.

Deas and the junior class gained a lot of experience during their sophomore year. They were now the alphas of the school. Jeremy Kennedy would start at point guard and Gabe was poised to start at the two. Deas was now 6'2" and had developed a good inside-outside game. Gabe's brother A.J. would start at forward, and Joey Cash would man the middle.

District 4A was always known as one of the strongest districts in the state, but this year it was stronger than ever. Every team was competitive, but everyone knew 'The Big 4' would own the district again.

Lookout Valley had a good group of seniors and a talented class of sophomores that included our old friend Keith Galloway. CCS had the most talented player in the district in 6'3" swingman Willie Lucas, and 6'10" junior Dave Dennison, who could step out and shoot the 3-ball along with Phil Jacobs' group of sophomore tough guys.

Boyd Buchanan had a seasoned starting five that was the perfect combination of mean, tough, talented and together. Everyone in the district hated them for it, just as much as their fans and student body loved them for it. And their fans were crazy. They always had a small group of students who sat behind their opponent's bench and waved a giant flag during the games. This flag was so distracting, because it would randomly graze the top of your head during the time-outs. Dad would get so salty about that stupid flag and have words with those students nearly every time we played. I'm pretty sure they liked the attention. The rest of their wild student body would sit across the gym. Each time we played them they had one fan that took it upon himself to be my own personal heckler.

He wore a red t-shirt with 'Temple #3' spray painted across the front and 'daddy's boy' spray painted on the back. He came to the games with a baby pacifier in his mouth and a small bib around his neck that read 'daddy's little man.' They had great organized chants too. Whenever one of us would get called for foul, their entire student section would shout out in perfect intimidating harmony, "You boy! You boy! You! You! You!" To this day, I have never seen a more ruthless high school student section.

At every big district game, the gyms would be packed with rowdy students, so Lefty would sit in the bleachers on the other side of the gym across from the benches. Fortunately, his voice could carry over the vuvuzelas at a 2010 FIFA World Cup match in South Africa. Our ears were trained to hear his instructions on one end and Dad's on the other.

By Christmas we were playing well, and I had earned a significant role off the bench as a 3-point shooting specialist, playing 8-10 minutes per game. If Jeremy or Gabe got in foul trouble, I played more. If they didn't, I played less. I usually took one or two shots. They were always 3's, and I knocked down a high percentage of them. During one stretch mid-season, I made a 3 in seven consecutive games, which was a pretty big deal considering I never took more than two 3-point attempts in any of those games.

Gabe and I had been showing great improvement throughout the year, due to the experience we had been getting. Gabe's confidence level was rising and he became our second best scoring option behind Deas. My minutes had gone up as well, as a result of my efficiency from behind the arc. You would think that with so many players in one class that the team would have been cliquish, but that wasn't the case at all. To my knowledge, there was no pettiness. Everyone shared the ball and got along great. However, this didn't mean that all the parents liked the young pups playing a significant role on this team.

Any coach playing his son is going to be controversial, so of course Dad had been taking some heat because I had been getting varsity minutes. But, it wasn't like I was starting or anything. I only played half the game at the most, and rarely took more than two shots. I didn't turn it over and was always in the right position on defense. Dad never gave me anything. I always had to earn everything I had gotten. So far, I had earned my place on this team and I knew it.

Dad wasn't going to punish me or the team over a few upset parents. He was confident in his coaching and didn't need validation from anyone. He would put his team in the best position to win the game. End of story. But he did coach me slightly differently than everyone else. The difference was primarily the lack of public praise.

Around mid-season, Dad called me into his office one day before practice.

"Josh, I know it's probably hard to play for your Dad," he said, "and I'm sure it's going to get even harder. I just want to make sure you understand a few things."

"Whatever you earn on the court, you'll get. If you earn minutes, you'll get minutes. If you earn the bench, you'll get the bench. I know you wouldn't have it any other way."

"I won't punish you on the court for being my son. I won't reward you for being my son either. People will always talk and say crazy stuff. We just gotta block out the noise and do our work."

"But I want you to know ahead of time that I'm not gonna give anyone any fuel for their fire when it comes to us. Because you've set a high standard for yourself, I'll probably be harder on you than most. And, I hate to say it, but because you're my son, I'll probably be harder on you than most. I'm not gonna try to be; just know that it'll probably happen. I'm just human. You're skilled and you've worked so hard to get where you are now, but I probably won't say many good things about what you do in front of the team. That's just how it has to be. There'll probably be times that you think it isn't fair. Just know I'm not trying to be unfair. No matter how hard I may be in the gym, when we get in that car I'm just Dad. No matter how you play, no matter how many shots you miss, I'll love you the same and be so proud of the player and person you are."

I wasn't sure where all this was coming from, but—like any kid—I always relished hearing that Dad was proud of me. That was all I ever needed.

I found out later that he had received a scathing anonymous letter from a parent. The courageous author called him an idiot coach multiple times. He showed me the letter on the day I graduated from high school. I had no idea.

He told me, "Josh, throughout your life, people will try to hurt you. They will say hurtful things and it'll sting for a minute, but don't let it last any longer than that. They don't know you. They don't know why you do what you do. Should it hurt? Probably not. But when it is personal, it does hurt a little, no matter how outrageous the source. You just gotta let it go, and do your best. Don't let anyone that doesn't know you or love you hurt you for more than 5 minutes with their words. You have nothing to prove to critics that are gonna throw chin music at you simply because they don't like what they see in the mirror every morning. But if a friend or family member says something that hurts you, you'd better listen. They care and they are only trying to help."

Recently, Dad told me a story about his college roommate Bob Hetrick.

The summer of my fifth grade year Dad had one of his best little kid's camp turnouts of his coaching career. He ended up having 104 campers ranging from 1st through 6th grade. One of whom was Robert Hetrick. Robert was a tiny 1st grader who was the son of Dad's old college roommate Bob. When camp was over Dad took Bob to dinner before he and Robert would hit the highway to head back to Alabama.

"What a great turnout this week, Kevin," Bob said. "I can't believe how many kids you had in that gym. I have no idea how you managed teaching all of them so efficiently, but you pulled it off."

"Thanks Bob. I just hope the kids got better and had fun," Dad said.

"You know, out of the 104 kids you had there, you coached 103 of them so well," Bob said.

Dad was taken aback. "What do you mean? Is Robert okay? Did he not have fun?" Dad asked, thinking he was talking about Robert.

"Oh no. Robert had a great time. He doesn't

even want to go home," Bob replied. "I'm talking about Josh."

Dad didn't know what to say. I don't remember this occurring, but apparently, Dad had gotten all over me for missing the front end of a one and one during the final game on Friday.

"What do you mean by that? Bob." Dad said looking pretty annoyed.

"You got all mad at Josh about that free throw, but did you see all the great things he did this week?" Bob continued. "Kevin, he shoots the lights out, yet he is unselfish to a fault. He passes the ball to his teammates, even though some of them can't catch a cold. He already has a high basketball I.Q. and he sees the floor better than most of the guys on your varsity team. You're missing out on all the fun. It's not like he wanted to miss that free throw. You know, if you focus on his mistakes, I don't think you'll be able to coach him in high school, or worse, he eventually won't like playing."

Dad told me he was initially hurt by his friend's words. But these words came from genuine love, kindness, and concern. Bob knew Dad very well. Fifteen years after college graduation, these guys were still involved in each other's lives. This was a real friend, who was not afraid to hurt Dad's feelings to tell him something that would help him. Dad told me that this one conversation had an incredible impact on the way he would coach me in the future. It hurt his feelings, but he knew Bob was right. It made perfect sense. I am thankful that Bob was Dad's friend. My career may have been far less enjoyable if it were not for Bob Hetrick.

25

WE FINISHED THE REGULAR season 18-7. Boyd Buchanan had swept us during the regular season, and had beaten us for the third time in the District 4A semifinals by one point. They seemed to have our number. We would face Boyd again for the fourth time in the 'loser goes to the house' region semifinals. We had confidence going into the game because we nearly had them in the District tournament. We didn't wanna let them beat us a fourth time. Jeremy picked up his second foul midway through the first quarter, so I was called upon to play the most first half minutes I had played all year.

We were clicking on all cylinders working our inside-outside attack by pounding it into Joey and spreading the floor with made threes. I was having my best game of the year when it mattered most. I had hit

2 threes on 3 attempts in the first quarter, and we had a 6-point lead with the ball on the opposite baseline with three seconds remaining in the first half. Boyd was pressing to try to force our young guards into a turnover and score a cheap basket before the time expired. A.J. was inbounding the ball as Gabe flashed in front of him only to be double-teamed. I darted the other way, and A.J. threw me the ball near the free-throw line. I was on a full sprint toward our basket. I took two dribbles, and Chris Tally reached for the steal. I anticipated his gamble and took the ball behind my back, took one more dribble, and launched a prayer from half court. Swish. I couldn't feel my face. Maybe it was because of the adrenaline or maybe it was because A.J. had put me in a celebratory headlock as we were heading off to the locker room. The crowd was going crazy, and we had taken a 9-point lead into halftime.

There had never been any love lost between Temple and Boyd. The two small Christian school rivals hadn't necessarily played nice in the past. There was no one we would rather play spoiler to their dream season than Boyd Buchanan.

Boyd came out for the third quarter with a three-quarter court 1-3-1 press with 6'5" swingman Chris Jones at the top. His arms hung down to his knees and he was causing all sorts of chaos getting deflection after deflection. We slowly began to crumble against their press. By the end of the third quarter, Boyd had taken a 1-point lead, and they would never look back.

Me as a 110-pound freshman handling a trap from Boyd's Bopper Coppinger (50) and Chris Jones (right)

This Boyd group was special. They were old heads that possessed a will to win that set them apart from everyone in our district. I guess it set them apart from everyone in the state because they went on to win the state championship in Murfreesboro that year.

We finished the season 20 and 10 with four of those losses against Boyd Buchanan. We had never been owned so hard by one team. It was a bitter pill to swallow, but it made us all the more motivated for the 96-97 season. We were ready to prepare like never before. Individually, I was hell-bent on earning a starting spot. That didn't concern Dad though. His priority for me was to make sure that I stayed healthy over the summer. He also wanted me to start being a man since I would start driving this summer, so he made me get a job. My cousin Nathan was working on the grounds crew for the Minor League baseball team in town, the Chattanooga Lookouts. They had another opening, so I went with him to apply for the job, and I got it. Dad was ecstatic that I would have a job that would keep me from putting too many hours in the gym. It was the perfect job for a high school kid. We would take care of the field at the historic Engel Stadium and get to hang out with professional baseball players all day. Many of whom were only a few years older than us.

Since I was only going to be able to get into the gym 4 days a week due to my job, I developed the most intense workout I had done to date. It started with some ball handling drills for a warm-up, followed by a 600 shot game speed workout. I would never use a rebounder which would allow me to work on my conditioning as well. When I finished my 600 shots, I would do a strength shoe work out to improve my quickness, explosion, and vertical jump.

Our team rolled through the summer team camp season. We played in four weeks of team camp that year and split up our teams for two of them. The other two weeks we played the biggest schools in North Georgia. We didn't lose one camp game the entire summer. We had size, shooting, experience, and were the toughest team every time we walked onto the floor.

Fortunately, I grew two inches over the summer. On the first day of school, I was a massive 5'8" 125-pound juggernaut, ready to rock and roll.

26

SEPTEMBER 9, 1996. MY classmates and I were shuffling around Dad's classroom talking about the high school issues of the day while we waited for him to come in and teach our U.S. History class. As the bell rang, Dad walked into the classroom, and everyone found their way to their desks. Dad was a great teacher, but he was an even better storyteller, so U.S. History was the perfect class for him to teach. He loved history because he could share lessons we could all learn from the great men and women who came before us. That day, he would tell us another story, but this story wouldn't be about a great battle. It wouldn't be about our forefathers. This story was about personal history. Dad's history. It was the story of my brother Mitch (Higgs), who had been born 11 years before on September 9th, 1985.

I knew the situation surrounding Higgs's birth and the

events that followed because I lived it, but I didn't really KNOW the story. I didn't know Dad's story.

He took a seat on his desk and began to tell a story that would change my life.

"September 9, 1985. My wife Vicky and I were living in Lima, Ohio and had two perfectly healthy children, and she was expecting our third. We were at our house when Vicky told me it was time, and I raced around the house in a panic. I went into Josh's room, broke up he and Rachael's game of G.I. Joe's vs. My Little Ponies, tossed them over each of my shoulders, and ran out the front door with a pair of little feet kicking around each side of my face. Vicky was already in the passenger seat with tears in her eyes from the combination of contraction pains and excitement. She started to laugh when she saw my stereotypical Dad move.

'This is it Kevin. Our family will be complete. I just can't wait to hold our new little boy,' she said on our drive to the hospital.

It never crossed our minds that there could be an issue with the health of our third child. This was the 80's. There were no 3D ultrasounds, and the doctors often didn't catch something wrong with the baby while he was still in the womb.

When we arrived at the hospital, the nurses could see that it was time to deliver. They wheeled her off to labor

*and delivery, and I went with her, leaving Josh and Ra-
chael with the babysitter who had just arrived.*

I told her she was gonna do great.

She said knew she would. This wasn't her first rodeo.

*When the baby came, something seemed off. The doc-
tor was being very gentle handling the baby. We all had
masks on, but you could see the fear in his eyes. He looked
at the nurse and said something I couldn't make out. They
let us look at the baby. Mitch was the most beautiful baby
you've ever seen. The doctor had him carefully positioned
so we wouldn't see his back. Then they took Mitch away.*

*We waited for the doctor in that room for 20 min-
utes. It seemed like three hours. Nobody would tell us
anything. The doctor finally came in and gave us the
dreadful news—Mitch had been born with an open spine
condition called Spina Bifida, and would need emergency
surgery to close the opening in his lower back. He told
us that our baby was currently on a helicopter on his
way to the University of Toledo where they specialized
in this type of operation. Vicky was sobbing. I was doing
everything I could to keep it together for her sake, but I
was crushed. I asked him some questions about what we
should do next. Before the doctor left the room, he handed
Vicky a Polaroid picture of Mitch."*

As Dad continued to speak his voice began to crack
and big tears started to stream down each side of his face.

I looked around the room at the faces of my somber classmates. The moisture in my own eyes was growing to a blur, and my breath was getting shorter as I was fighting a breakdown with everything I had. My classmates had never seen me cry and I didn't wanna start now. The girl sitting next to me had full tears running down each cheek, and you could begin to hear the sniffles and sobs from all corners of the room.

"I watched her as she looked at the Polaroid. She started to crack a smile through the tears. She looked up at me and said, 'Kevin he's so beautiful.' "

He paused for about 10 seconds trying to collect himself.

The room was dead silent.

Then he whimpered,

"She just wanted to hold her baby boy."

Nearly every kid in the classroom was now openly crying—full blown crying—especially me. I couldn't keep it in anymore, nor did I care to.

He continued to tell us the story about Higgs' journey through life. Higgs had nine surgeries in the first two months of his life, and fourteen by the time Dad was telling us the story. The doctors told my parents he would probably never walk, and their lives would change drastically. But when Higgs was three years old he took his first steps, and he currently walked around the school like any other kid. If you didn't know his story, you would not even suspect that he had a condition.

There was a lesson in every story Dad told in the classroom. His point that day was that no matter how tough life gets, God is good and He will see you through the hard times. To me, it was much more than that. I now understood why Dad possessed such a good perspective on life. He didn't take anything for granted. He loved us with all he had. Best of all, he possessed the uncanny ability to let the things that don't matter truly slide.

Before I heard the story, I would hold a slight grudge against Higgs at times, because in my eyes he was Dad's special boy, and I was always the one getting in trouble and taking the brunt of Dad's discipline. It felt like Higgs could do no wrong. Looking back, it might have been because he IS one of the best people I know and always has been. After hearing the story, I would never see my little brother in the same way again. I have never met one person who did not genuinely like him. Higgs was born with some disadvantages in life that were out of his control. He was born the son of a basketball coach, and the brother of two successful athletes, but he never got to take one shot or hear the crowd roar for him. However, to this very day, I have never once heard him complain or wallow in self-pity about his plight. He loves life and everyone loves him.

Despite his physical disadvantages, Higgs is blessed

with one particular social advantage that contributes to the person that he has become. Higgs didn't grow up immersed in a world of high competition. He never had the urge to compare himself with those around him. Because of this, he became a master of empathy. He celebrates the successes of those close to him like no one else in the world. He shows genuine interest in everyone's story and makes them feel like a million bucks. For as long as I can remember, he has had the ability to carry on conversations with complete strangers for hours. When people leave a conversation with Higgs, they don't leave thinking about how great Higgs is. They leave thinking about how great they are. After hearing that story, I found myself so proud to be my father's son as well as Higgs' brother, and all of our first world high school problems didn't seem so big that day.

Higgs

27

THE WEEK BEFORE OUR first day of practice my sophomore year, three of our senior starters (Danny Deas, Jeremy Kennedy, and Gabe's brother A.J.) were expelled from school for a violation of school rules. They had been seen drinking alcohol by a few parents and a teacher at a local amusement park. Drugs, alcohol, and smoking were big no-no's at our school and were cause for immediate expulsion. Our team had really high expectations for the upcoming season, and this was a huge blow.

I felt so many different emotions that day. I felt bad for them and I was angry with them at the same time. I also felt bad for Dad. Because of his character, he had risen to the position of Dean of Students at the school. He had to do his job, and I know that the situation was difficult for him since he loved them and had invested so much into their lives.

Selfishly, I had been looking forward to competing for a starting spot. I didn't want to be given a starting spot, I wanted to earn it. I wouldn't get that chance now, but I had to move on. Those guys were gone, and we had no control over that. Practice was starting, and we had work to do. Our goals wouldn't change, so the next man would have to step up.

Dad held a 2-day open tryout on Monday. Nearly every boy in the school showed up to try out, sensing the opportunity to step into the program after the loss of our three starters. The gym was packed. Dad decided to use this opportunity to see if there was anyone in this group of aspiring Temple hoopers that was tough enough to make the team. First, we stretched out and did some ball handling warm up drills. After we finished our warm up, Dad put twenty minutes on the clock. He had everyone line up across the baselines of the two side courts. He placed industrial sized trash cans in the corners and on each side of the half court line.

"There are twenty minutes on the clock," Dad shouted across the gym. "When the clock starts, you will start running sprints. Every twenty seconds you will hear a whistle blow. That means you will jog for the next twenty seconds. If you have to walk, then walk, but when you hear the whistle blow again, open it up and sprint. And so on, and so forth until the clock hits triple zeroes."

Dad was going to see if it was worth it to someone. Us returners started smiling at each other. We could run for days, so this was not anything new to us. We knew what he was doing. The clock started and all 40-plus of us took off in a dead sprint. It looked like a mini Boston marathon inside the Vance gym. Slowly but surely, the new guys started dropping like flies one by one. By the 10-minute mark, nearly every trash can had a newbie doubled over it. A few guys even started hiding behind the bleachers, hoping Dad wouldn't notice after they had blown chunks in a corner can. It was hilarious. When the buzzer finally sounded, there was only one new guy standing. My new classmate, David "V" Casteel. He was a hard-nosed military kid who had probably lived in 10 different cities. His father Carlos was a green beret and became a sergeant major in the army. I guess toughness was in his blood.

It may seem like this was cruel and unusual punishment, but, hey, it was the nineties. Guys seemed harder back then. It was just understood that if you were going to play in this program, you had to be another level of hard.

Our new starting lineup was me at point guard,

senior 3-point specialist Matt Neal at shooting guard, Gabe on the other wing, senior big body Aaron Mc-Guirt at the 4, and Joey Cash in the middle. Juniors Ricky Gossett and Braucht Walters would play a significant role off the bench. We got off to a blazing start and went into Christmas break 10-2 with some big non-district wins already under our belt. I was playing well at the point. I had prepared myself that summer to run the show, so the varsity game had slowed down for me. Gabe was having a breakout year scoring the basketball. He was too big for the guards to handle and too fast for any big guys to guard. Dad had morphed the offense around the strength of Gabe as a scorer and my playmaking and shooting ability. It was working and we were looking like one of the strongest teams in the region.

During Christmas break, Dad always gave us at least a week off to get away from the game, recharge our batteries, and spend time with our families. He was intentional about keeping us fresh during the long season. Toward the end of our first practice back, I got a steal during a scrimmage and raced the ball to the other end. Braucht was chasing me down as I went up for a layup. He took a shot at the ball and I lost my balance in the air and fell awkwardly on my ankle. CRACK! I fell to the ground in intense pain. As I rolled around on the floor, the gym fell quiet (sans my groans of course). Braucht stood over me trying to help me up in hopes that I was okay. I know he felt terrible, but it was a clean play. Sometimes, bad things just happen. Dad came over and asked how bad it was. I told him I thought it was bad. I had never felt pain like that before. Gabe and Braucht helped me to the bleachers.

Practice continued as I iced my ankle on the bleacher. I could feel the blood rushing down, and it felt like my heartbeat was coming from my ankle. I knew I would be out for a while and was crushed. I just stared off into space in utter disbelief of what had happened. Sure I had been injured before, but I could usually play through it and had post season surgeries. I had never missed a game.

Our team was devastated as well. When a player gets seriously injured, it is like all the air gets let out of the gym. Dad could see that nobody—himself included— wanted to be there anymore, so he called practice after five minutes.

I was experiencing some serious self-doubt and couldn't help but question the durability of my body. I'd had two surgeries and now probably a broken ankle in less than four years. *Am I just brittle? Am I going to be one of those guys who just stays hurt? Will I even get the chance to find out how good I could be?* By the time the guys broke it down at center court, my ankle had swollen to the size of a softball.

When Dad and I got in the car, I broke down and cried. Our team was good. I was finally a starter and was having an All-District caliber sophomore year. I was having the time of my life, and just like that, my season was over. Dad tried to encourage me, but I was so distraught I don't remember anything he said on that ride home.

The next day we went to the doctor to get x-rays. It was a third degree sprain with a clean break of my ankle bone. I was looking at six to eight weeks for recovery. The season was over in two months so I was pretty much done. The silver lining was that I wouldn't need surgery, but sadly, it was time to dust off the old crutches.

When Dad and I got in the car to go back to school, he knew this was a low point for me. He tried his best to help.

"Josh, I know you feel like this is the worst thing that could happen to you. There are worse things that could happen, but I understand how you feel. I wish I could take the pain away, but pain is part of life. The difference between the hard and the soft is how we respond to painful circumstances. Tough times make tough people. With the right mindset, you CAN become a better player because of this."

"How is this going to make me a better player, Dad?" I said in a frustrated tone.

"Maybe not physically, but you're young. You'll recover," he said. "But it could make you so much better mentally. There is something about seeing the game from a coach's point of view that makes you a better player and better teammate. Your basketball I.Q. will get better too. It'll be like you're part of the coaching staff for rest of the season."

From that point on, I sat by Dad on the bench during games. When we got in the car, we were game planning. It was a 15 minute daily coaches meeting on the ride home. I think at first he was just trying to make me feel included, but it did work. And he was right. After watching the game like a coach, I could see the game in a new light.

Before my injury, we rarely talked about basketball on the car ride home. He was never coach when we climbed into whatever nasty rig would take us home, he was Dad, and we talked about our day. After my Elementary and Jr. High games, he would tell me how much fun it was to watch me play, celebrate a specific play or two, or that he was proud of me, nothing more. I am sure that if I lived through the horror story car rides home that some athletes tell, I would've developed different feelings about the game. I was never worried about Dad picking apart my every move in the car, which I'm sure allowed me to play with a clear head. Looking back, I realize how much this practice empowered me. At the time I thought it was a completely standard practice for fathers of athletes, but now, I realize now how special those car rides really were.

28

OUR TEAM WAS GETTING used to the 'next man up' philosophy. Braucht stepped into the starting lineup. He struggled at times, but he was gaining valuable experience and getting better every day. After going 2-2 to start second semester, we would play South Pittsburg High School for homecoming. It was a capacity crowd in the Vance gym, and we jumped all over the Pirates that night. We took an 18-point lead into the halftime break. With 6 minutes left in the game, we were up by 28 when Dad took out the starters. After the St. Anthony game 3 seasons before, Dad loved the idea of having a point forward. He always wanted a big man that could bring the ball up the floor and relieve the pressure when our guards were being harassed too much. A big guy is usually always guarded by the other team's big guy who is not great at full court defense on the ball. In turn, bringing it up shouldn't be too difficult for a point-forward who has a good handle. With me hobbling around on crutches and holding down my new job as assistant coach, this concept was even more valuable. The best guy to play the role of point-forward for us was Ricky Gossett. Ricky had the skill set, but not the experience. He wasn't quite ready for the role, but this would be a perfect time to get him valuable experience handling the pressure. For the best coaches, every opportunity is valuable, and there is no such thing as 'garbage time.' However, players often have a hard time grasping this concept.

When we emptied our bench, South Pittsburg decided to put on the press. When Dad saw this he called time out. He wanted Ricky to be our primary ball handler against the press. He pulled out the clipboard to make sure that all the guys were in the right spots on press break so they would be available if Ricky found himself in trouble. Ricky struggled against their press. His mistakes started to snowball, and he probably had 5 turnovers in the quarter. South Pittsburgh cut the lead to 20 but would get no closer. When the final horn sounded we shook hands and made our way to the locker room.

Dad had all the guys standing in a circle around

him while he congratulated us on a game well played. We all had our eyes locked on him as usual when we heard some noise coming from the lockers behind us. Dad paused and I looked over toward the lockers to see Ricky sitting down, taking off his shoes, and putting them in his bag. In our program, you never took off your gear or messed with your shoes until Dad was done speaking to the team. It was a respect thing. You gave him your full attention every time he was talking. Ricky was breaking one of our cardinal unwritten rules. In the past, Ricky had always been nothing but respectful. He was a quiet guy, a great teammate, and extremely coachable. He was just having an adolescent moment of temporary insanity.

"Ricky, do you have somewhere to be?" Dad asked.

Ricky replied with anger in his voice, "Yeah, anywhere but here."

"What?" Dad was stunned.

"Coach, you put me out there to play a position that I don't play just to embarrass me in front of all those people," he shouted. "I'm sure everyone got a good laugh at my attempt to play point. Thanks a lot, Coach."

As he was getting the word coach out of his mouth, Gabe, Aaron McGuirt, and I were simultaneously yelling for him to shut up.

He did shut up. You could hear a pin drop in the locker room as Dad slowly walked away from the huddle toward Ricky. Dad looked like he was about to explode. He reached down and picked up one of Ricky's shoes from on top of his gym bag. Everyone stood in silence with no idea what would happen next.

"Where did you get these shoes, Ricky?" He asked as Ricky dropped his head and started staring at the floor. "Who bought them for you?"

Ricky said nothing. Knowing full well he had let his ego and feelings get the best of him. He knew he had crossed a line that was never to be crossed. Dad had always taken care of Ricky. Ricky, much like the rest of us at Temple, came from a blue collar family, but Ricky's parents didn't care about his basketball career. So Dad became like his basketball father. If he needed a ride home from practice, Dad gave him one. If we had a game back to back on a Friday night and Saturday afternoon, Ricky would stay the night at our house. If Ricky couldn't afford gear or shoes, Dad took care of it. We all knew this, which made Ricky's outburst shock us even more.

"Where did you lay your head last night? Where did you eat breakfast this morning, Ricky?" Dad continued. These questions were purely rhetorical.

"... The people you love the most are the only ones that can hurt you."

Dad was obviously wounded by Ricky's lashing out. I think he was even more wounded because in that moment Ricky did not trust him.

Dad turned and threw the shoe as hard as he could against the side lockers. It made a loud bang that echoed in the completely silent room. The volume of his voice crescendoed with every word.

"I put shoes on your feet. I take you into my home. My mom cooks you dinner. You eat my cereal in the morning. The Cinnamon Toast Crunch was gone by the time I got to the table. Who ate that? You Josh?" he asked, lightening the moment as he turned and looked at me.

Propped up on my crutches, I sheepishly shook my head. Like any loyal friend would do when interrogated by his father, I pointed at Ricky. Everyone, including Ricky, tried to hold back a snicker. We weren't quite sure if it was safe to laugh.

Dad's voice lowered, turning from anger to compassion, "I love you, Ricky. You're like a son to me. How could you not trust me after all we have been through? There is a bigger picture than just tonight. You've gotta understand that."

"I'm sorry, Coach." Ricky said.

I was so relieved that Ricky fell on his sword and

apologized so quickly. He knew he was wrong when he was lashing out, but his feelings just trumped his logic and sanity for one short moment. The room stayed quiet as Dad told Ricky to get back to the huddle with the rest of us.

"Ricky, I understand why you felt the way you did. I should've communicated why I did what I did better, but you gotta trust me," Dad said.

He scanned the eyes of each player around him. "This goes for everyone in this room. This type of disrespect is something that happens once. Not once for Ricky... once for everyone. If it happens again, you will not be a part of this team. Am I clear?"

"Yessir," Everyone said without hesitation.

"There is a reason behind everything I do. You have to trust me. If you don't trust me or you don't trust your teammates, then don't come to practice on Monday," he concluded. We broke it down, and everyone exited the tension filled locker room with a sense of disbelief about what we had just witnessed. There was also a sense of relief that it was over.

29

WE STRUGGLED DOWN THE stretch of the regular season and entered the tournament with a 19-8 record. I was making the most of my new assistant coaching role by taking in everything Dad and Lefty would say. My ankle was ahead of schedule. Rehab was going great, and it looked like I would be cleared to play just in time for the tournament.

We won our district tournament quarterfinal game in convincing fashion.

Next, we would play Lookout Valley in the district semifinals. It would be my first game back. I was eager to play again and help the team any way I could, but my ankle wasn't near 100%, and Lookout Valley was very good that year. Keith Galloway's class was now seasoned juniors. Their depth and athleticism proved too much for us to handle as they ran away with a double digit win. I felt like a shell of myself and played awful. My timing was off, and the quickness and explosion I had before was non-existent. It was painful in more ways than one. I thought my return could give the team a shot in the arm, but instead, it had the exact opposite effect. My rustiness and limited mobility seemed to hurt the team.

Dad had always taught me to get outside myself and do what is best for the team, but it was hard. I'll admit that I had a hard time getting outside myself a few times during my career, but deep down I always wanted what was best for the team. On the ride home Dad asked me how my ankle felt. I told him it didn't feel good, and that I just didn't have any speed.

He said he could tell I didn't look like myself, and told me that my role would be limited to the role I had in 9th grade (stationary shooter). He would use me if we needed some shooting, but we were going to have to go with the other guys most of the game. Of course I didn't like it, but I accepted it. I knew he was right. I just wanted to win and help the team any way I could, even if that meant embracing the difficult task of sitting on the bench and being a great teammate.

In the first round of the region tournament, we would face off against the best team in the neighboring region, Knoxville Catholic High School. They controlled the action the entire game. We made a few runs, but couldn't get over the hump. I played a little, but still struggled. As much as I wanted it, the bottom line was that my ankle just wasn't ready.

Despite losing 3 starters before the season and another over the Christmas break, we finished with a 20-10 record. The same record that we had the previous year. Our guys battled to the end and Dad was extremely proud of what this team had accomplished through all the adversity.

30

AFTER THE PREVIOUS YEAR'S tournament disappointment, and my less than stellar comeback attempt, I never wanted to feel small and slow again. That's the worst feeling you can have on the basketball court. It was hard enough being 5'8" and 125 pounds, but to feel slow? Being slow makes you feel even smaller.

Dad had always told me I needed to add one thing to my game every off-season. This year that one thing changed my game—a jump shot. Dad's old Ohio coaching buddy Marc Dalton had convinced the both of us that, for me to have a chance to play in college, I would need to change my shot. Because I would always be small, I needed to be able to get my shot off quicker and have a higher release point. It would also allow me to be much more effective shooting the ball off the bounce.

Dad always told me, "If you can shoot, I mean really shoot, every defender you face will be off balance when you look at the rim. This will make you a faster basketball player."

Logic told me that if I have a quick, high release, my defenders would be even more off balance. How fast would I seem on the court then? Lefty said the name of the game is speed, so I was all in on the jumper. Coach Dalton and Dad came up with a plan that involved many reps from short distances during the first month. I didn't shoot one shot outside of 10 feet for THREE WEEKS. I bought into Coach Dalton's philosophy of repetition being the path toward mastery. Dad was pleased because my workouts were pretty low impact on my body. He rebounded more for me during that summer than he ever had in my life. I had to get up reps in high volume, and he was always there to lend a helping hand. It was a boring and tedious process, but by the end of April I had a sweet new jump shot, and this new J would add a whole new dimension to my game.

I was still working at Engel Stadium, but I made sure I would get in the gym either before or after work. It would take me about 90 minutes to get up my 600 shots. I did the same shooting workout 6 days a week for the entire summer. Every day after my shooting workout, I would spend 30 minutes in the weight room to work my core and upper body, or I would do my strength shoe work out for quickness and explosion.

By the time the camp season rolled around, we had our five starting spots pretty much set in stone. Braucht Walters came on strong toward the end of last season and was penciled in to start at guard. He was a 5'7" bulldog who never tried to do too much on offense and loved nothing more than harassing an opposing guard with his pesky full court defense. He would often get under their skin as well, which was something he seemed to enjoy. He was one of those players that you love when they play on your team, but you hate when you're playing against him.

Ricky had worked his way back into Dad's good graces. He was playing as well as anyone on the team by tournament time last year. He was a fast 6'1" lanky forward who was a quick leaper. He was wiry strong enough to bang with the big boys down low, and had also developed a consistent outside shot. Gabe and I would hold down the other guard spots. The final starting spot went to the last man standing from the conditioning tryout the year before, 5'10" wild man David "V" Casteel.

Our chemistry was off the charts at both ends of the floor. In the spring, Dad had put in a 1-4 high guard oriented offense to capitalize on me and Gabe's scoring ability, as well as Ricky's ability to play away from the basket. The offense fit our personnel perfectly, but the strength of this team was our suffocating pressure defense. When the five of us were on the floor, it was tough for the opposition to get a shot off much less put one in the basket. The next season looked promising… we just needed to stay healthy.

31

PRESEASON CONDITIONING WAS UN-DERWAY. A few guys opted to run cross country. They probably felt like punishing themselves over the Tennessee hills on a daily basis in the fall would be easier than a week of conditioning with Dad and Lefty in the gym. To each his own.

After coaching us at camp all summer, Dad had a good handle on our identity. This team had the ability to break wills on defense. This was the team he had dreamed of. We had four starters under six foot and Ricky. Coming off the bench, we had 5'6" speed demons Lance Walters and Jeron Williams, who were in the 9th and 8th grades respectively. Our first substitution for a post player was Joel Money. We weren't very deep so we needed to learn how to bring the heat by moving our feet. That would keep our starting five out of foul trouble.

In the TSSAA, no teams could practice with a ball before November 1st. For the last week of October, Dad handed our preseason 'conditioning' over to Lefty. For 90 minutes a day we slid up and down the floor. Fast slides, low slow slides, wall sits, 1 on 1 zig zag drills without a ball, and any other defensive stance drill you can fathom. We also worked on our full court and half court off the ball positioning. By the end of the week, we were in the best shape of our lives, and guarding would be our primary focus. We didn't just want to beat teams. We wanted to break them.

Our first game was against my old neighborhood pal Tripp. Tripp had moved to Chattanooga to go to school at Notre Dame High School. We always wished we could play together, but it was just not meant to be. We jumped all over them hitting 7 threes in the first half. Our hot first half shooting had spread them out, and we got 6 back door layups within the offense in the second half. The offense had a counter for every defensive adjustment they tried to make. I had a big game, posting a career high 28 points, and we won 75-50. Dad was pleased and he told us if we stayed true to our defensive identity, we could win games without shooting well. When we did shoot well, the games wouldn't be close.

I knew it was just the first game, but something felt special about the guys in that locker room. Most of us had been playing together since the 7th grade, and our chemistry was great at both ends of the floor. We had been through a lot together—injuries, trust issues, disappointment, and conditioning to name a few.

The culture Dad was building at Temple was about team, celebration of others, humility, and shared success.

Complete trust and togetherness seemed to fill every inch of space in our locker room. There was no room for ego. There was no room for pettiness. There was no room for anything less than total buy-in to Dad, each other, and our culture. This team had no size, no big time college prospects, but we had heart, passion, love for each other, and toughness. We would ride those qualities as far as they could take us.

32

THAT YEAR THE TSSAA split the legendary District 4A up into two districts. Everyone was sick of having the best 4 teams in the region in the same district. So old District 4A would now become Region 3A. Boyd, Grace, and Temple would be the main players in the new District 5A. CCS and Lookout Valley were the main players in the new District 4A.

CCS's good group we battled in Jr. High was now all seniors. They were joined by the best young basketball prospect the city of Chattanooga had seen since Porter Roberts; 6'4" freshman sensation Jason Holwerda (who later started at Vanderbilt).

Lookout Valley had one of their strongest teams in school history. Keith Galloway and his senior classmates were tough, and Keith was at the top of his game. He went on to be All-State in three sports that year, basketball, baseball, and football. There has not been one athlete in the history of Tennessee High School sports to have ever accomplished that feat. Valley had a healthy crop of young talent as well. The best prospect of them all was 6'5" stud athlete Sidney Pointer. Sidney and a few of their other players had all grown up playing in Highland Park, and Gabe grew up in Lookout Valley. We had played with or against these guys since the fourth grade, and there was a lot of familiarity and respect between our teams.

Our first big region game of the year was a Tuesday night home game against Valley. The first half was a back and forth affair. In the first possession of the second quarter, Keith attempted to make an entry pass to the wing. I anticipated his pass, jumped the lane, and slapped the ball toward the half court line. We both sprinted toward the ball. He beat me to it and picked it up with both hands, toeing the half court line. I slammed on the brakes, but not soon enough. I swear I barely touched him, but his momentum was already going that way, and it didn't take much to send him across the line. And send him I did. He went flying to the ground across the half court line. Keith was 5'11" and probably weighed about 185 pounds. He made it look like he had been hit by Lawrence Taylor. The ref whistled me for my second foul. I looked sideways at the ref, then glared at Keith. He was looking back at me with his patented Galloway joker smile. It was my second foul and I would be making my way to the bench.

"You savvy dog. I'll get you for that," I said, as he bit his lip in an attempt to keep from laughing. That son of a coach was a savvy dog, but as much as it made me mad, I could respect that. Most coach's sons are.

When I got to my seat between him and E.Z. (our new assistant coach who was also a longtime friend of our family), I started to explain to Dad how bogus the call was. "That was so weak. I bar—"

Dad stopped me right there. "Shut up, Josh. You can't change the call. So shut up about it. You put yourself in that position."

"But, I—" I was cut off again.

I really wanted to tell him that I barely touched him. Dad never was much for excuses or explanations about mistakes, especially from me.

"But... nothing. You knew you had one (foul). You gambled and lost. You put it in the ref's hands. Never put your game in someone else's hands," he said.

He was right. I was reminded of the wise words from Dick Devenzio I had heard at Point Guard College.

"Take responsibility for your game every time. If something goes wrong, it isn't someone else's fault. It's you. There is almost always something you could've done

better. If you get fouled and it's not called, don't complain or whine to your coach or the refs. Don't get fouled! Make a move so strong that a foul can't stop you. Make a move so quick that a defender can't get to you in time to foul."

Dad continued to let me have it on the bench. "Now you will sit here for the rest of the half. You guys have to learn that every foul is a mistake. If our defense is as good as it can be, we won't need to gamble. We won't need to foul. We will just always be there because of our feet and our positioning. It's the one silly foul that gets you in trouble. The sooner you figure that out, the better."

We went into the half facing a 5-point deficit. Gabe had the same issue in the second half. He picked up a silly second foul reaching for a steal 60 feet from the basket early in the third quarter. It seemed meaningless at the time, but became relevant when he picked up a blocking foul on his attempt to take a charge on the same possession. It was a bang-bang play, and the call could've gone either way.

Dad never argued the call. Instead, he just sat there waiting for Gabe to make his way to my old seat between himself and E.Z. I'm sure Gabe got the exact same speech. I ended up fouling out of the game, and the strength of Valley's team proved to be too much for us to overcome, with me and Gabe spending so much time on the bench. They left our house with a 62-56 victory, handing us our first loss of the season.

The lesson Gabe and I learned in the loss against Lookout Valley would be one of the most important lessons we could learn while playing on this team.

"It is the silly fouls that get you on the bench. Even if they may seem meaningless at the time, they are the ones that get you," Dad said to the team in the locker room after the Valley game. We all knew we needed everyone in our starting five on the floor as much as possible. The gap between our starters and our bench was too big. Lance and Jeron were always ready when called on, but they were pups. Joel had not quite grown into his body. He would grow to 6'3" over the summer and become one of our most valuable players the next year, but he wasn't ready yet.

On Friday, we would travel across town to take on CCS. For some strange reason they invited us to their homecoming game for the second straight year. For the second straight year, we were happy to play spoiler to their homecoming festivities. Our defense stifled the usually sure-handed chargers by forcing 21 turnovers and holding them to 31 points.

By mid-December we were 6-1. School was out for the holidays on Friday December 19th, but we wouldn't be taking our break quite yet. We would travel to Knoxville to play in a four team holiday tournament. In the opening game, we would play Midway—a big class A team from middle Tennessee. During the pregame warm-ups, a group of Midway players started laughing at us at the other end. We were taught to never look down at the other end during warm ups. Our focus was on our task at hand, not our opponents. But, this time it would be impossible to ignore the sneers of our opponents. Every time one of us would approach the end of our layup line at half court, one player from Midway would greet us with a cutting remark.

"I didn't know we were playing a Jr. High team today," he said to Gabe as his teammates chuckled.

"Did Mommy bring your juice box?" he shot in my direction.

It was like this dude was trying to come up with new insults each time he went through his layup line. I'll give him credit for his smack talking game. He was bringing it. There were two problems though, first, he needed a little more game to back up his mouth. Second, you know that kid in the school yard that your Dad always told you to stay away from because he was just bad to the bone, and he might just beat you mercilessly if you messed with him? Yeah. We were that kid. We never said anything back to him. We just smiled and let him keep digging his own grave. After they announced the starting lineups, our starting five huddled on our side of the center court circle.

Braucht took the lead. It was like Dad's words were coming out of his mouth. "I know you guys heard all that too. This guy doesn't realize what he just did. We'll let our game talk. Let's climb all over 'em. Don't let 'em breathe."

We were all on the same page. This game was over before it ever started. Dad called off the dogs after three quarters. We were up 53-18. They had more turnovers than points. The next day we avenged our region tournament loss from the year before against Knoxville Catholic 67-42 to take the holiday tournament championship, and took an 8-1 record into the break. Only two of our opponents had made it to 50 points.

Braucht's suffocating defense

33

AFTER THE BREAK, WE would pick up right where we left off by convincingly winning two more games in Johnson City, Tennessee. Next on the docket would be District 5A play. We opened district play on a Tuesday against the Golden Eagles of Grace Academy. Gabe's stellar defensive effort frustrated their best player Albert Curtis, holding him to only 4 points as we claimed a 58-29 victory.

On Friday, we would travel to District rival Boyd Buchanan. The young Bucs of Boyd crumbled under our pressure as we ran away with a 52-28 win. One week later, we would face one of our biggest tests of the season. Our not-so friendly neighborhood powerhouse McCallie.

McCallie was having a big year as well. They had one of the best inside-outside attacks in the city. The combination of junior guards Jay Lookabill (Navy standout Ryan Lookabill's little brother), and Andy Campbell with dominating 6'8" big man Justin Huntley made them a force to be reckoned with. It was a Friday night and our homecoming crowd filled the seats and spilled out into the corners, forcing the fire marshal to close the doors.

The game was an instant classic. It featured 12 ties and 15 lead changes. We had the ball trailing by 2 points with 12 seconds on the clock. Gabe threw the ball to me as I came off a screen on the wing. I ripped the ball through and drove by Campbell on the baseline. I felt contact from him on my shoulder as I took it to the basket. I immediately jumped for a shot through the contact. The ball rimmed out as Campbell was whistled for a foul. With 2 seconds on the clock, I would be going to the line to shoot the potential game tying free throws. It never crossed my mind that I could miss. I stepped up to the line and knocked down the first one. The crowd roared. I took a step into the lane and exchanged fives with Ricky and Gabe. Before the official could toss the ball to me for my second attempt, McCallie head coach Steve Carpenter called timeout.

We had already practiced what to do at the free throw line in case of a miss in a late game situation. Dad knew that Ricky and Gabe knew what to do. He only talked about how we would defend the final two seconds after I made the free throw. It felt like he thought that was the only possible outcome. He always had us prepared for late game situations by playing one and two minute games in practice every day. This allowed him to just give us reminders and instill a little extra confidence when the pressure was at its highest. It was an effective tactic.

I confidently stepped up to the line for my second free throw. I took my usual three dribbles and let it fly. It felt great but bounced off the back rim. My heart skipped a beat as Huntley reached for the rebound. Gabe shot into the lane, stuck out his paw, and reeled the ball in, smack dab in the middle of a cluster of bodies. As he went up for the put back, Jay Lookabill got a piece of his arm. The whistle blew, and the clock stopped with .2 seconds remaining. Everyone went nuts. Our fans were nearly on the court hugging and giving high fives. Gabe had my back. He willed the ball out of the crowd. Though it helped that he had a pair of the best hands in high school basketball. Gabe stepped to the line and knocked down both free throws as we went on to win 55-54. Our students stormed the court. This was the biggest regular season win in school history.

On the Monday after our exhilarating homecoming win over McCallie, we arrived at practice more confident than ever. This time, however, our confidence manifested itself in a different form. It wasn't the healthy kind of swagger that leads to hard work and toughness. This was complacency. We had started to read our own press clippings. We started the day going through the motions of our warm up drills. Next up would be press break games. During these games our cuts were not as sharp, and we were uncharacteristically careless with the basketball. For a brief moment, we had lost the abnormally large chip on our shoulder that made us who we were. Dad was becoming more and more frustrated. After back to back turnovers in a mini game, Dad had seen enough. It was time for him to remind us of our identity.

"Get out!" he shouted. We began to jog toward the sideline.

"No. Not out of the game. Out of the gym!" he declared. "You guys must think you are really good, but what have you done? Which one of these banners in the rafters did any of you guys hang? This is the most uninspiring basketball I've ever seen from you guys."

Our starting five dropped our heads in shame as we headed to the locker room. As Gabe and I were about to walk in, Dad yelled at us from the sideline.

"Gabe, Josh. You better get this fixed soon or you'll be in for a big disappointment this year."

He always made sure we knew that it wasn't about his demands. It wasn't about his coaching career. It was about our aspirations. He knew what we wanted for our team and he was committed to holding us to our goals and the standard we set for ourselves.

We would fix it without needing to say a word about it. The point was made. He reminded us of our identity, and there would not be another bad practice in Vance gym the rest of the season.

Braucht, Rick, and Gabe got in their cars and took off. Just my luck, I rode with Dad to school that day and would ride home with him after practice. Just V's luck, he needed a ride home. We waited for Dad in the locker room, dreading the trip.

When practice was over, the rest of our teammates entered the locker room. Joel saw us sitting there and said, "Ooooh. Y'all are riding home with Coach? Sucks to be you." Everyone chuckled.

We were sure that Dad would let us have it on the way home, but that wouldn't happen. As always, when we got in the car, he wasn't coach anymore, he was Dad. He asked Higgs and Rachael about their day at school. Rach had a few funny stories from the day, and they laughed the whole way home. V and I just sat there in an awkward silence.

The next day we would drive twenty miles up

I-75 to play a district game against Charleston High School. We extended our winning streak to 12 games with a 53-23 win. The next two practices would be two of the best all year. On Friday we were more than ready to face region rival CCS and claimed a 65-54 win. This would put us at 16-1 on the year going into next week's tough Friday and Saturday road match ups at Lookout Valley and Arts and Sciences.

We lost a hard fought region game against Valley. Arts and Sciences had recently had a boost in enrollment and had moved up to AA. They had a huge front line in the 6'8" twin towers, Kenny Mobley and Justin Cambric. They were both game changing rim defenders, and we had a hard time getting anything near the basket. Our legs were tired since the five of us had pretty much played the whole game the night before, and it seemed every outside shot we took came up short. We fought hard, but received a good old fashion beat down by the Patriots.

Woody Hayes once said, "Nothing cleanses the soul like a loss." He was right. You see it all the time. A team rolls through the regular season undefeated and enters a tournament as heavy favorites to win a title. Then they suffer a devastating season ending loss. The 2014-2015 Kentucky Wildcats in college basketball, the 2002 Miami Hurricanes in college football, and the 2007 New England Patriots all come to mind.

Teams learn much more through losses than wins. We were overpowered by the size of Mobley and Cambric. The next time we faced a front line with that kind of size, we would be more prepared, because of what we had learned through the loss. Dad had intentionally scheduled these two tough games on the road on back to back days. He wanted us to be tested and ready when we would face back to backs against our toughest opponents in the tournament. He was always thinking two steps ahead.

Our souls must have been cleansed thoroughly, because we reeled off seven straight wins to close the season. In five of those seven games our opponents failed to score more than 27 points. The writers at the newspaper were starting to get into the spirit of things with their articles. Our defense was a rare experience to behold.

Dick Cook of the Chattanooga Free Press wrote: *There are some things you can depend on. The sun rising every morning. The love of a good dog. Jammed traffic on I-24. Tennessee Temple's defense.*

Stephen Hargis of the Chattanooga Free Press wrote of our thrashing of an athletic South Pittsburg team: *It was basketball's version of a train wreck. You had a grisly scene with plenty of carnage, but at the same time it was hard not to crane the neck and watch it all.*

We would take a 23-3 record into the district tournament.

Dad managing a timeout

34

WE HAD WON THE regular season District 5A championship, and would meet rival Boyd in the district championship game. Our defense had stifled the Bucs in our first two meetings, holding them under 30 points in both games. Boyd coach Ricky Perry was one of the savviest coaches in state, and he was determined to not let me or Gabe beat them. They opened the first quarter in a triangle and two on us, but Ricky Gossett threw a monkey wrench into his game plan that no one saw coming. He drained three 16 footers in the first quarter, forcing the Bucs to come out of the triangle. It was a tight game in the first half and we went into the break with a 21-18 lead.

We turned up the heat in the second half, and Boyd started to throw the ball everywhere. Boyd's guards were so eager to get rid of the ball that they would throw it to anyone. They didn't discriminate either. They tossed the ball to us many times, and even threw it to the official scorekeeper twice. Our constant pressure was too much for the inexperienced Bucs, and we ran away with a 54-32 win and took home the District 5A championship. Gabe led the charge with 24 points and was named District 5A tournament MVP, and Braucht and I were selected to the All-Tournament team by the Chattanooga Sports Writers.

Higgs was now 12-years-old. He was always part of the team, holding down my old childhood job as manager. Few people loved Temple basketball more than Higgs. When we won the district championship, he was one of the happiest guys in the locker room. He was in the back seat riding home with me and Dad from the game when he asked if he could see my All Tournament plaque.

"Josh, that was awesome. Can I see your trophy?" he asked from the back seat.

"No," I said.

Dad was understandably shocked by my response. "C'mon man. He's just a little kid. Let him hold the trophy," he whispered, trying not to let Higgs hear.

"I don't have it."

"What? You left it in the gym? Let's go back and get it," Dad said.

"No. I mean I don't have it. I gave it to Ricky. He deserved it more than me. He was the difference in the game. He came right out and hit those shots that knocked them out of the triangle. We need him scoring the ball, and this might give him a little extra confidence for the rest of our tournament run."

...understanding the meaninglessness of a painted gold piece of plastic was more important than my need for some validation. But there was even more to it than that. He wanted me to be the best TEAMMATE I could be. He wanted me to be a true leader who had the whole package.

This was a microcosm of how Dad raised me. It wasn't about accolades and trophies. It was about the team. Dad told me later in life that this was his proudest moment as a father during my career.

The region tournament was held 20 miles up the road at Sale Creek High School. After rolling through the first round, we would face our arch nemesis Lookout Valley in the biggest game of the year. It would be a do-or-die matchup of two teams ranked in the top 10 of the TSSAA state power rankings, with a combined record of 50-7. Someone would move on to the Region final and a berth in the sub-state, and the other would go home to dust off the old ball glove. Our two regular season losses to the Yellow Jackets did not sit well, so we would be out for blood.

Gabe had abused every opponent who attempted to guard him all season long. All but one, Lookout Valley's C.J. Taylor. I think the pressure Gabe put on himself to perform well against his hometown rivals had more to do with his struggles than Taylor's defensive prowess, but I'm not taking anything away from Taylor. He was a great defender, but Gabe had done work on bigger and better.

Gabe was one of my best friends. We had been playing together for years and we knew each other's thought processes. We wanted this more than anything in the world. Before we loaded up the van to head to Sale Creek, I felt the need to call my friend out, and get in his head. We sat in the locker room after a short pre-game practice and packed our bags for the game. From where I was sitting, I could sense Gabe's nervousness. Gabe was usually fearless, but this match-up seemed to have him slightly on edge. We needed our ballsy leader now more than ever.

I stopped packing my bag and said, "Gabe, why are you scared of C.J.?" I knew he wasn't afraid of him, but I wanted to make him mad, thinking maybe he would take out his anger on C.J.

He cocked his head as he glanced back at me. The

brashness of my question had taken him by surprise. "Well, I don't know, Josh," he shot back sarcastically.

"Well don't be, we're winning this game tonight," I replied.

"You know I ain't scared of him," he said. "I just don't know what it is about Valley. They've had my number."

"Since when?" I answered, with frustration in my voice. "Think about it. You had one bad game at their place. You're not allowed to have one bad game? When we played them the third game of the year we were both in foul trouble. That's why they beat us. Not because C.J. shut you down. Not because we played poorly. We watched too much of the game from the bench. Don't make it more than it is."

"You're right," he said.

"I think you're the best player in this city, and I'll believe that no matter what happens tonight. We may not shoot great tonight, but we don't have to," I said. Gabe was nodding his head, as if he wanted me to continue my pep talk. I glanced at Braucht and V in the corner. "Braucht and V would love nothing more than to beat them 30-28. All we gotta do is lock 'em up and dog them out the door. That's what we do."

I continued to preach as I got a few 'Amens' from the corner. "We can win games solely with our D. That should take all the pressure away. Let it all hang out and play free, bro!"

"We're gonna make them wish they told their parents and girlfriends to stay home," Gabe said to us with a sinister grin on his face.

That was the Gabe swagger I was used to.

35

W E WALKED INTO THE gym at Sale Creek with a job to do. As we sat and watched the first half of the girl's semifinal that preceded our game, in walked Valley. They had a swagger of their own. I'm sure they were confident—having taken us to the wood shed twice, but in a little over an hour they would become the unsuspecting victims of our bad intentions.

In the first half, they couldn't breathe. I denied Keith the ball, full court forcing their other guards to bring it up against the relentless pressure and speed of Braucht and V. The turnovers began to mount. We jumped out to a 10-3 lead by the end of the first quarter. They had more turnovers than shot attempts. The second quarter was more of the same as V and Braucht dogged the life out of them. Keith was starting to get frustrated and was demanding the ball, but I was always there.

Throughout the course of the season we would feed off of the frustration of our opponents. When they would start snapping at each other, we would energize. When they showed their frustration with their body language, we were like a pack of sharks that smelled blood in the water.

The halftime score was 20-9. Mighty Lookout Valley, with all the king's horses and all the king's men, dropped a nine spot in the first half. We didn't shoot the ball particularly well either, but like we had discussed in our locker room before the trip, we didn't have to.

The second half picked up right where the first had left off. With 3 minutes left in the game, Lookout Valley raised the white flag of surrender and emptied their bench. Dad followed suit. The crowd behind our bench was losing their minds as we walked off the floor. We exchanged hugs on the bench and breathed a sigh of relief. Gabe had violently thrown the monkey off his back as he dropped 24 on C.J. We were guaranteed at least two more games. That was the best part of it to me. We were still alive! I had so much fun playing basketball throughout my career, the thought of a season being cut short was my biggest fear. Sure I wanted to win championships, but most of all, I wanted to play more games and was so happy that our run would not end that night.

When the final horn sounded, we lined up to shake hands. Dad always reminded us to be gracious and carry ourselves with class before the hand shake. As we moved through the line, our dejected friend Keith hugged me and Gabe. He told us he would be rooting for us to win it all, and that it was an honor to compete against us. He was a class act and had an amazing career.

The following night we would play CCS in the region finals. We carried our defensive momentum from the Valley game over, and jumped out to a 10-0 lead right out of the gate. CCS coach Eddie Salter called a timeout, and the Chargers would regroup. As I mentioned before, it is always tough to beat a good team three times, but, by the end of the third quarter, we held a 39-31 lead, and it looked like we may do just that. But this CCS team wouldn't go away. They made a furious fourth quarter comeback and took their first lead with 2:37 remaining.

With 15 seconds left in the game we found ourselves down by two with the ball. Braucht inbounded the ball to me as I dribbled up the right sideline to run a play that would bring Gabe off a staggered screen near the top of the key. He caught the ball in the middle of the floor on a full sprint and drove to the basket with his strong hand. My defender had no intention of helping off me and giving up a kick out for a game winning 3-point attempt. Gabe put his head down, took it to the rack strong, and was hacked in the act. With 5 seconds remaining, Gabe would be heading to the line to shoot two shots. The ice in his veins came through again as he calmly made both to tie the game at 49. CCS called timeout and Coach Salter drew up a play that would put the ball in the hands of senior Phil Jacobs to make the final play. The night before, Jacobs hit a running 15-foot jump shot at the buzzer for their tournament life, sending Boyd Buchanan to the house.

Phil came off two screens, looping in front of the inbounder and receiving the pass on a dead sprint that veered straight toward our basket. Braucht was sprinting beside him in an attempt to get in front of him and slow down his forward momentum. Jacobs crossed our 3-point line in 4 dribbles as he rose up to shoot a 16-foot jumper over Rick's outstretched hand with Braucht riding his hip. The buzzer sounded while the ball was still in the air. It touched nothing but net. CCS had won the region crown 51-49. It was a well-played game by both teams. Kudos to Phil Jacobs. That dude was clutch.

The loss was disappointing, but we were not dead yet. It was time to bounce back. We would have to travel 3 hours upstate to the sticks of 'Nowhere,' Tennessee, to face one of the toughest teams we would face all season, Clarkrange High School in another do-or-die game. The winner would move on to play in front of thousands of basketball junkies from all over the state on the biggest stage in Tennessee high school basketball... the TSSAA state tournament at Middle Tennessee State University's Murphy Center.

36

O N MONDAY WE HEADED up to Clarkrange
to play for our school's first state tournament
berth since 1992. Dad wanted us to get there early so
we could familiarize ourselves with a gym that we had
never played in. Our bus pulled into a full Clarkrange
parking lot at 5:00pm. We grabbed our gear and
walked into the gym. I could not believe what I saw.
The stands were already two-thirds full, two hours before tip-off.

Dad looked at me and said, "These people must be
serious about their basketball."

It was the understatement of the year.

During warm ups we were getting heckled by their
student section about our size. It was pretty standard
stuff, and they weren't even particularly clever, mostly
just cliché. I heard all the 'daddy's boy' noise that I

usually heard. By tip off, the fire marshal had closed the doors because gym was packed to capacity. We had a section of about 200 supporters in a corner by the lobby doors. The atmosphere was downright rowdy.

We got off to another fast start, and I was on fire. It all started when I threw a baseline inbounds pass to myself off the back of Clarkrange big man Scott Hall for a layup. I think he was mad about me throwing the ball off his back, because on the next possession he caught the ball on the elbow, took two dribbles, and threw down a vicious two handed dunk on Ricky. Their crowd went ham. I'll admit, it was nasty, but we still had the upper hand and took a 34-25 lead into halftime. I had 18 points and zero fouls going into the locker room.

The third quarter started with my picking the pocket of their point guard Casey Gunter and taking it in for an uncontested layup. Our pressure was starting to get to them until a few whistles caused us to back off a little bit. I was called for a foul when I bumped Gunter while turning him near the sideline. It was just my 1st foul, no need to worry. My 2nd foul, however, was totally unnecessary. On the ensuing inbounds pass in front of our bench, Gunter caught the ball going away from his goal. As he turned to take his first dribble, I measured him and took a shot at the ball. It was a classic case of greed. I lunged and picked off his dribble while bumping him in the process. The whistle blew for my 2nd foul. Dad had a disgusted look on his face, but I thought to myself, No big deal it's just my 2nd foul.

"...every foul is a mistake. If our defense is as good as it can be, we won't need to gamble. We won't need to foul. We will just always be there because of our feet and our positioning. It's the one silly foul that gets you in trouble."

This one would come back to haunt me. The crowd roared on every whistle that went against us, and the officials seemed to be getting into the home-town spirit. I would get my 3rd foul in the third quarter on a block/charge call that didn't go my way.

Gabe had started to heat up in the 3rd, and we had a 49-39 lead going into the fourth quarter. But they had a run left in them. We couldn't seem to keep them off the line. They shot 28 free throws in the second half alone. It felt like we were in handcuffs, and couldn't so much as breathe on them. V and I had four fouls apiece with three minutes remaining. We still had an 8-point lead, but they had started to full court press, and our team needed us on the floor.

I would be the first to go. Gunter tried to drive into the lane, but I cut him off before he could cross the free throw line. He picked up his dribble, looked at the rim, and made a nice shot fake. I was certain he was shooting and I left my feet to contest the shot. I jumped straight up while he stayed on the ground. I could see it coming and tried to throw my hands back while I was in the air to avoid the foul. He jumped straight into my stomach Kevin Durant style. The whistle blew.

"You put it in the ref's hands. Never put your game in someone else's hands."

I was stunned. A stupid, silly foul had done me in again. This time it was when it mattered the most. Braucht's little brother Lance checked in for me. He stuck out his hand to give me five as I passed. I grabbed his hand, put my other arm around him, and said. "This is what you've been working for. You got this. Be confident and get us to state."

He looked so nervous, which made me even more nervous as I walked toward the bench. Dad was salty.

He just glared at me as I walked by to my seat. He didn't say a word. He didn't have to. I felt terrible.

V fouled out on the next possession. They had all the momentum, and we were just trying to hang on at this point. We were up one with 8 seconds remaining when they fouled Gabe. He would go to the line and sink both free throws like he had done so many times before. We were up 3. Clarkrange called a timeout to set up a final 3-point attempt for the tie. In the huddle, Dad instructed the guys, "Braucht, it's probably coming to Gunter, so keep him in front and don't let him catch the ball going toward their basket. Everyone else, don't let him pitch ahead, and don't help off the arc."

Braucht did exactly as he was instructed. Gunter had to run toward the inbounder to receive the pass. He turned to take it up the floor. Braucht was with him step for step and made him change direction twice. Gunter went back to his right hand and threw up a highly contested prayer from 30 feet out. The ball went in off the glass. The building was shaking. It was so loud you couldn't hear yourself think. We would be going to overtime.

We had already lost two starters in regulation. Things were not looking good, but Gabe had other plans. In the overtime period, he put us on his back, literally carrying us to Murfreesboro. He was a one-man press break taking the ball coast to coast many times. He made one high degree of difficulty shot after another.

My boy Joel Money came up big as well with two huge steals down the stretch. With 45 seconds remaining, Joel jumped into a passing lane and intercepted a wing entry pass. He was flying down the floor for a layup when he was fouled hard from behind by

Gunter. Joel lost his balance and fell on his right hand, breaking one of the bones. Joel was from Highland Park though. He wasn't going to let a broken hand keep him from stepping up for his team. He went to the line and drained the first one. His hand had already started to swell. He looked at it, looked at the bench, and cracked a big smile as he stepped up for his second shot. He banked it in. Guess it was meant to be. Gabe scored 11 in the overtime and finished with a career high 38 points as we ran away with it 84-75.

All 200+ of our traveling fans spilled out onto the court when the final horn went off. It was a great celebration, and Dad let us have all of it. We exchanged hugs and cut down their net. Even Lefty was out on the court like Jimmy V looking for people to hug. There was no post game speech from Dad. He just wanted us to enjoy each other and our fans. He was always big on having us show personal appreciation to the Temple Fans. At least once a year after a big win he would have us go into the stands and thank everyone instead of going into the locker room for a post-game speech. This time the fans came to us.

After about 30 minutes, we went in to get our gear out of the locker room and loaded up to head home. Gabe still had the net around his neck, and the celebration continued on the bus. For 5 minutes, while the driver waited on everyone to load up, there was a mosh pit going on in the back of the bus that was literally rocking it from side to side. Players, J.V. guys, managers and cheerleaders were all in on it. Dad just sat up front and smiled as we had our fun. Buy the tickets—book the rooms. We were going to state.

Lefty found someone to hug

37

THE EIGHT TEAMS THAT make it to the state tournament are matched up by a blind draw at the state tournament coach's meeting, and—of course—we drew #1 ranked Donelson Christian Academy. Donelson was 30-4 and didn't have a starter under 6'2" which meant their point guard was taller than Ricky, our lone post player. They were led by 6'8" Adam Sonn. Adam was the winner of the TSSAA class A 'Mr. Basketball' award, and after high school, he went on to become Belmont University's all-time leading scorer and 2-time Atlantic Sun Conference player of the year. He averaged 28 points and 16 rebounds per game during his senior year at DCA. They also had 6'4" bouncy forward M.J. Garrett, who averaged 16 points and 8 rebounds per game. He would go on to start at wide receiver for Vanderbilt in college. DCA was one of the highest scoring teams in the state, and we held our opponents under 36 points per game. Something would have to give. We had our work cut out for us, but we kinda liked work.

Legend has it that DCA's coach Tommy Frensley gave Keith's dad Joe Galloway a call to get a scout on us. Coach Galloway told Dad about this conversation before we left for Murfreesboro.

"What is with these guys? They're tiny. They only have two guys that really want to shoot. I know your region is tough. How did they win so many games?" Coach Frensley asked Joe.

"Man, it's hard to explain. They get into you like no one I've ever seen before. I mean they held our guys to 9 points in the first half of the region semis. And we had a really good team!" Joe replied.

"So they press and rotate a lot of guys and break you down?" Frensley asked.

"No. They only sub if one of their starters gets in foul trouble. Which isn't often. They pick you up man full court and are just always in your face and in the passing lanes. You feel like they're fouling, but they aren't. At least the refs don't call it. They just move their feet," Joe said.

"Well, they may be good defenders, but I don't know how they'll get a rebound against us. Our starting lineup is 6'8", 6'4", 6'4", 6'2", and 6'2"," Frensley continued.

"Well, Coach, I see only one problem. You gotta be able to get a shot first," Joe replied.

Everyone who gave Dad a scout on DCA told him you had to pack it in with a zone around Sonn and make them shoot threes. We hadn't played one possession of zone all year. That was not us. We could only be who we were.

"When you are taking your dog to the dog show, if it's a pit bull you can't try to make it a collie. Even if we are the mutts of this dog show, we'll be playing like pit bulls," Dad told Stephen Hargis of the Chattanooga Free Press.

Our bus pulled into the Murphy Center 90 minutes before tip-off. We walked into the bowels of the arena straight to our designated locker room, wearing our shirts and ties. The massive locker room was nice and smelled like Downy dryer sheets. Which was a nice change of pace from our locker room at Vance. It smelled like mildew and death. We took our time putting on our gear, soaking in every moment of Division 1 locker room luxury that we could. Dad had his old buddy Marc Dalton, who was mostly responsible for my new jump shot, speak to us before we took the floor. Coach Dalton spoke to us from the Bible, Ecclesiastes 9:10, "Whatever your hand finds to do, do it with all your might."

It was almost time as we left the locker room and walked through the cold cement floor hallway to the tunnel. The lights got brighter as we stepped out of the tunnel like a gladiator at the coliseum. The squeaking sneakers, whistles, and roar of the crowd were deafening, and my heart was nearly beating out of my chest. The clock struck triple zero and reset to 15:00. It was our time to take the floor.

Playing in the arena in front of thousands of fans was a rush. Many of Dad's former players from Temple and Ohio showed up to show their support. I had never played in a place this big, or in front of a crowd this big. In the first half, everything I threw toward the basket was long. Maybe it was the adrenaline. Maybe it was the open arena background at the Murphy Center. Whatever it was, it didn't matter. We brought the heat. We ran off to a 15-8 lead at the end of the first quarter. Gabe guarded Sonn by fronting him and using his speed to beat Sonn to every spot on the floor. Sonn was the best post player we had ever faced. He had baby soft hands and a deft touch. If he caught the ball, he usually scored. He just didn't get the ball very much because we pressured their guards into turnover after turnover. When they did look for him inside, we put intense ball pressure on the passer, and Gabe was in front of him with help behind him. There was usually another one of us on his top side, just waiting to get a hand on any entry pass that was attempted.

At the start of the fourth quarter, we had a 34-32 lead. DCA's players had started showing their frustration by bickering at each other. That's when we knew they were close to breaking, and break them is exactly what we did in the fourth quarter. Gabe scored eight of his game high 26 points in the fourth quarter. He also held Sonn to just 11 points (17.5 below his average). We forced them into 25 turnovers for the game and won the fourth quarter 17-4. The final score was 51-36. One of the newspapers called it David over Goliath. Coach Frensley of DCA said that we played the best defense he had ever seen in his long coaching career.

Surrounding Sonn

Dad had become somewhat of a media darling since he had been at Temple, but the writers were really enjoying his wit on this run. He always gave them a clever one liner that would be perfect for print. We probably got more than our fair share of newspaper coverage as a result. The boys ate up his one liners like a kid eating candy on Halloween night.

A few of his greatest hits were:

"We're not pretty, but we're gritty."

"If we are Cinderella, this princess wears work boots."

"Defense has been our business all year, and business is good."

Dad calling the plays

The state semifinal was a train wreck if there ever was one. We played against 8th ranked Oneida, and they had size as well. The strength of their team was their big guards 6'2" Derek Lawson and 6'2" Adam Jones. Oneida was the best half-court defensive team we had played all year. They gave us a taste of our own medicine in the first half, holding us to only 14 points. They focused on keeping me and Gabe from getting any clean looks at the basket, but we didn't allow them any clean looks either. We took a 14-6 lead into halftime that left their coaching staff just standing on the court scratching their heads. Lefty told us later that they stood out there for five minutes trying to figure out what to do. Oneida's 6 first-half points were the lowest total allowed in a half in state tournament history. When we got in the locker room Dad joked that blocking their extra point after the touchdown could be the difference in the game. He urged us to keep guarding and told us our shots would eventually fall.

We kept them at arm's length for most of the game. Gabe started to get loose in the fourth quarter, scoring 8 of his game high 21 points. Their frustration was visible which made us come at them even harder defensively. It seemed every time one of them would actually get into the paint, one of us would step up and take a charge. We took six charges in the game. With 2:30 remaining in the game, Derek Lawson drove into the lane, and I stepped over and took what would be his fourth charging foul. It would be his 5th total foul which would send him to the bench. He was clearly frustrated, and began arguing the call with the official as he stood up. As he continued to plead his case, I got up from the floor and said, "Just go have a seat, big boy." The whistle blew. Oops. I would be popped with a technical foul for the first time in my career.

Braucht, who was usually the team hot head, took off in a dead sprint over to Dad and said to him, "Coach, it wasn't me." Thanks Braucht. I looked at Dad... he was fuming.

My mouthiness didn't do Gabe any favors as Oneida's frustration would simmer to a boiling point. No more than one minute later, we had the game in hand when Oneida big man Heath Phillips dropped his shoulder like a linebacker and lowered the boom on Gabe who was dribbling at full speed across the center court line. Our guys took exception while Gabe was still on the floor trying to regain the breath that was knocked out of his lungs. Cooler heads prevailed, and both coaches emptied the bench. We went on to win 42-29, advancing to our school's first ever state championship. It was the 10th time that we had held our opponents under 30 points.

Swarming Defense by V (left), me (center), and Braucht (right)

A Happy Bench

Ricky

Gabe

Chattanooga Free Press Shot

38

THE STATE CHAMPIONSHIP. IT is the game that every kid in Tennessee imagines they are playing in while shooting in their driveway. It is the game where one team's dream season is capped off by hoisting the coveted golden ball, while the other is dealt the biggest heartbreak of their career. Never in my wildest dreams did I think I would be playing for Dad in this game with my closest friends in front of 8,000 basketball fans. It was surreal.

On paper we shouldn't have even been there. We had one of the smallest teams in the state, from one of the smallest schools in the state (133 out of 135 in Class A according to enrollment). Fortunately for us, basketball is not a game that is played on paper.

We would square off against Ezell-Harding from Nashville. Like DCA, Ezell's strength was their size.

They were led by 6'6" versatile forward Gerrod Shirey, and 6'1" point guard, Ron Sarver.

Looking back, I should've been more nervous to play in a game of this magnitude, but when basketball is played for pure reasons, the nerves have a tendency to stay on the shelf. As we stood around the jump ball circle, Michael Buffer could be heard shouting, "Let's get ready to rummmbbbbllllleeee," straight into the jock jam stadium anthem, *Get Ready for This,* over the PA. The student sections were losing their minds in their respective end zones. I felt a feeling of euphoria as the adrenaline pumped though my veins.

The ball was tipped and the rest of the game was a blur. It felt like I was outside my body. I let go, threw myself into the moment, and played purely on instinct. The game played out just like the Holyfield/Bowe fight we had watched in Highland Park years earlier. Both teams were throwing haymakers in an attempt to score a big knockdown, but the heart and the defense of both teams overcame every time. After and 8-8 opening quarter, we held them to 3 points in the second, taking a 16-11 lead into halftime. Neither team had made a substitution.

No matter how good of shape you are in, three games in four days is tough for high school bodies, especially when you rarely sub. Although you couldn't tell by the effort each team was giving, the legs of both teams were starting to go. You could see it in jump shots that were usually drained at a high percentage falling short for both teams. This game would be decided solely on heart and determination, and neither team would come up short in that department. We continued to control the pace of the game and took a 24-21 lead into the final period. The Eagles tied the game at 28 with 1:30 remaining, but Gabe would respond with a floater in the lane twenty seconds later. Ezell ran their offense patiently looking for the game tying score. Gerrod Shirey caught a pass from Sarver off of a pick and roll and was fouled with 18 seconds left. He hit both free throws. With the score knotted at 30, we would come down the floor to get the final shot at winning it all in regulation. We ran the dribble entry double screen for Gabe and he caught the ball heading toward the meat rack. As he went up the ball was slapped out of bounds by an Ezell-Harding defender. There were 2.8 seconds left on the clock.

Dad drew up a play where Gabe would inbound to me in the corner and immediately dive into the mid-post. If he was open I would quickly fire it in there. If not, I would have to make a play. I caught the ball in the corner, and as expected, Gabe dove inside. Shirey anticipated the post up and jumped on Gabe's top side, sticking his long arm in my passing lane. I saw this develop and reacted on instinct. I looked at the rim as if to shoot, getting Sarver to raise up out of his stance, then stepped by his hip and put up the shot as time expired. Everyone in the building held their breath. In and out. We were going to overtime.

The overtime period didn't have many possessions, so the value of each one was priceless, and neither team was giving up anything easy. The offenses were run methodically as both teams would seek out the ever elusive great shot. With 30 seconds left and the score tied at 35, Ezell would hold the ball for the final shot. They couldn't penetrate our defense. The ball never made it inside 15 feet, and they were forced into an off balance jumper at the buzzer. It wasn't close. Double O.T!

Shirey began the second overtime with a three and a difficult layup in traffic on back to back possessions. We were facing a 5-point deficit which was like being down 15 in this game. Our backs were against the wall. They held us at that distance until I hit a three to cut the lead to 2 points with 3 seconds left. Dad immediately called timeout. We had to have a steal. They had to inbound the ball against our crazed dogs who would be switching every screen. We were still in it. If any team could will it in this moment, we could. Ezell was out of timeouts, so they had no other option but to get the ball inbounds.

The official handed the ball to Ezell's Lucas McCain and began to count.

1... Sarver came off a screen, Braucht covered him up.

2... Shooting guard Lucas Graham came off a screen, I covered him up. The ref kept counting.

3... Another guard darted toward the ball. V covered him up.

4... McCain started leaning forward holding the ball directly over his head. Their guards started to dance frantically in a state of panic.

4.5... Shirey cut back toward half court and McCain launched it. Joel was right with him. It was like wide out vs. cornerback going after a jump ball in the back of the end zone. Joel would try to tap the ball back to our end with his rubber cast on his fractured hand. They both leaped as high as they could. They met at the top. Shirey tried to reel the ball in with one hand as Joel took his shot at it. He slapped the ball and it deflected off Shirey's hand and toward the Ezell-Harding student section. I watched helplessly from our free throw line as Joel ran after the bouncing ball as hard as he could, with Ezell's student section jumping around in the background in a state of celebration. The image will be forever etched in my memory. I fell to my knees as the buzzer sounded. It was over. I looked to the side-line thinking, *I'm sorry Dad. I tried.*

The season was an amazing ride. We finished 30-5 and state runner up. It was the best season in school history, but that did nothing to take away the pain of that moment. The Ezell bench stormed the floor and mobbed their players on the court. While they were jumping around in jubilation, I was still on my knees trying to hold back the tears with my head down staring at the hardwood. I felt a tug on the back of my jersey. Gabe was trying to pick me up off the floor. I stood up. He put his arm around me as we walked toward the bench.

"You're my brother," he said, as we walked.

I couldn't say anything back. I was about to lose it completely. Braucht and Ricky met us half way over there. Me and Gabe glanced at the Ezell players celebrating.

"Don't look at that," Braucht said. "All that matters is right here."

He huddled us up around the 3-point line in front of our bench. I was now officially weeping in front of 8,000 people. We put our arms around the shoulder of the teammate next to us and leaned in to hear what Braucht was about to say.

"We have nothing to be ashamed of. We did what

people said was impossible, and we did it together. Let's hold our heads high. We can look in the mirror tomorrow knowing we did all we could," he said, while choking up.

As he was finishing those words, Dad jumped right into the huddle between Gabe and Ricky. He looked at Braucht, then Ricky, then Gabe, then me. Then he looked down, as if he was trying to gain his composure. There was a small puddle of tears on the floor in the middle of the huddle.

"Thank you. You guys inspired the entire state. Thank you for taking me on this ride," Dad said, as he looked at each one of us. Then he locked eyes with me.

"I've never been more proud of a team as I am of this one," he said, staring right at me.

In my heart, he was talking right to me. I knew he was talking to all of us, but I was his son. In that moment I knew he was proud of me most of all. I would trade a gold ball for that every year.

"Now, be what you've been all year. Be gracious in the interviews. Carry yourselves with class. Be proud, but be humble. Be you," he said. He never missed a teachable moment.

After all was said and done, we got in the car to make the 2-hour drive home. Mom was riding shotgun, and I sat in the back seat with Rachael and Higgs.

We all sat in silence for about 15 minutes. Dad finally broke the silence.

"Wow," he said.

I sat up in my seat.

"Wow," Higgs said. We all smiled.

For the next 2 hours, the five of us would celebrate the greatest hits of the season together. We told story after story—laughing and sometimes crying—the entire way home.

Dad working the sideline in the state championship

39

DAD HAD MADE A rule for me that I was not allowed to touch a ball for two weeks directly after the season. I was growing up, getting a little wiser, and had been through enough injuries to understand that I needed this rule for my own well-being. When the two weeks were up, I was rested and ready to work on my game. Gabe was gone, so I knew I had to step up my game. After a pickup game one Saturday, Lefty told me that I needed to 'own the arc' if I wanted to play in college. I was going to be a senior and couldn't conceive of my career ending after high school, so I took my workouts to another level. I got in the gym every day and attacked my game speed shooting routine harder than ever and had gotten up over 30,000 shots by the time the camp season started.

During the last few weeks of school, I would go

across the street and play pick up with the college guys. I was more than holding my own against them. I carried myself with a swagger and would never consider backing down from the college guys. We would go at it. I had competed against older, bigger guys my entire life, so why would this be different? A few of the college players took exception, and I got into a few physical altercations during these pickup games. It wasn't like this was new territory for me either because in Highland Park, the occasional physical altercation was standard procedure for high level pick up ball. I was gaining confidence every day and was ready to be the guy.

We lost a lot from our previous year's team, Ricky, Braucht, and our go-to guy Gabe, who had been named to the All-State team. Those three starters left big shoes to fill. During the spring, Joel had built on the confidence he gained with his late game heroics at Clarkrange. He would be counted on heavily to fill Ricky's shoes. That left us with two starting guard spots to fill, and Dad would let the summer decide.

Dad scheduled a few practices before our team would compete at TTU's team camp. As we were getting loose before the first practice, a slender, athletic looking kid walked in the door with his dad. His name was Caleb Marcum. His dad Scotty had taken an assistant pastor position at the church on campus, and Caleb would be enrolling in our school for his junior year.

"Who's that?" V asked me.

"I have no clue, but he looks pretty athletic. We can only hope," I said, knowing full well how young our team would be. We needed one or two more players.

Caleb grabbed a ball and we walked toward him to introduce ourselves. As we were approaching him, he put up a shot on one of the side goals. His form was nice, and the ball touched nothing but cotton.

I looked at V and smiled, "Sweet."

I had also talked one of my coworkers at Engel stadium to come play with us for his senior year. His name was Eric Kee. Eric was a 6'2" skilled forward who had taken the year off at a local AAA school because he had lost his love for basketball. I convinced him to give it another go, because he might just have the time of his life. He enrolled at our school during the first week of June.

Our young pups and new pieces seemed to be gelling at team camp. We rolled through the competition early in the week and would play Byne high school from Albany, Georgia on Wednesday afternoon in the McGilvary Gym. Our mentality had carried over from the year before. We wanted to break everyone with our defense. We were younger and had two new guys that were still getting used to Dad's defensive system, but everyone on the team had bought into the will breaking defensive mindset. Byne's kids were a different breed. If they couldn't beat you, they would try to beat you up. They couldn't do much about our defense with their game, so their frustration manifested itself in dirty play.

Dad was coaching some of the younger guys in a game across the street in Vance gym. He had left me and V to act as player coaches for this game, which he did often with his trustworthy older guys as a form of leadership training. We climbed all over Byne, and their guards had a hard time getting the ball across half court. We were up big late in the first half, when V went up to grab a defensive rebound. As he reached for the ball, he pulled a muscle in his back. He landed and went to his knees in excruciating pain with the ball under his arm, and his other hand reaching around to hold his lower back. A Byne post player shoved him to the floor and started to kick him when he was down. Of course I wasn't having any of that. I lunged in like 'The Macho Man' Randy Savage, flying off the top ropes. I threw every ounce of my 140 pounds into his body, knocking him backwards about five feet. The officials were players at the university; they knew us, and they knew this ugly scene could escalate quickly because we weren't backing down from anyone. The official closest to the situation was John Nelson, a stocky shooting guard who I'd always respected because of his toughness. John was yelling at me, trying to convince me to chill out and let the ref's get the situation under control. I started to calm down as the ball rolled out of V's hands to the feet of the dirty Byne big man. As Nelson was calming me down, the Byne big man threw the basketball like a baseball on a frozen rope right off my face from no more than 8 feet away.

All hell broke loose. I charged the mound. Nelson tackled me from the side and took me to the ground as I was losing my mind in a blind rage. Joel grabbed the Byne big man and started throwing punches. The Byne guy escaped his grasp and started backing up toward the lobby doors. Joel charged at him and they carried their fight into the lobby. The other official was trying to break up Caleb and one of Byne's guards. Eric was exchanging blows with the other Byne post player. It was like there was a separate fight going on in each corner of the court. Nelson still had me wrapped up on the ground waiting for more adult assistance. The game on the other court had stopped because of the commotion. The Byne coaches and officials from the other floor stepped in to defuse the situation. I guess it did escalate rather quickly.

V would have to go to the training room to get treatment on his back and would be out for the rest of the week. Joel got ejected along with two players from Byne. Things calmed down for the moment, and the game continued. But Byne wasn't done yet. With seconds left in the half, I got a steal on our defensive end and pitched it ahead to Caleb who was streaking down the sideline. A Byne guard looked like he was measuring his steps to try to block Caleb's layup attempt. He was actually measuring Caleb up for a clothesline hit across the head. He knocked out one of Caleb's front teeth. The joke was on him too though—he ended up with a deep 3-inch gash down his arm that was spewing blood all over the floor.

Nelson blew his whistle waving both hands. "This game is over. I don't get paid enough for this," he said.

The trainer had a pretty full plate after that game. Dad was called over to the gym. At first, he was angry with us, but when he found out that V had actually been hurt and was kicked while he was down, he calmed down a bit. Although he would never admit it, I think he was proud of us for standing up for each other. It was a crazy situation, but we learned a lot about Caleb and Eric. They had our backs like we had been boys since grade school. We had new brothers whose toughness would fit in perfectly, and I was excited about playing another season with a close-knit group of friends.

40

WE STARTED OFF THE 98-99 season like we hadn't missed a beat. I was shooting the ball well, and we darted off to a 12-0 start including a pair of 2-point overtime wins at Lookout Valley and McCallie. Our team chemistry hadn't missed a beat either since last year. Heeding Lefty's advice, I was owning the arc. The work I had done over the summer to perfect my jumper and quicken my release was paying off in spades. I was averaging over 20 points per game. With the additions of Caleb and Eric, we had more offensive firepower than the year before, and Jeron and Lance were coming of age at our third guard spot. They could pressure the ball effectively on defense, and spread the floor with their 3-point shooting.

In early January we would put our undefeated record on the line against Boyd Buchanan. They were now experienced seniors who were playing great basketball led by freakishly athletic forward Donnie King, who had become a dominant force in District 5A. We were down by 2 points at the half. Boyd had kept me in check, holding me to only 6 first half points, but I came out of the break on fire, knocking down shot after shot. But Boyd always had an answer. At the end of the third, Boyd still held a 38-37 lead. The fourth quarter saw many lead changes before Boyd took a 4-point lead with 2 minutes remaining. They made their free throws down the stretch and went on to hand us our first loss of the season, 61-53. I didn't know what more I could do. I had scored 29 points in the second half alone, missing only two shots.

After the game, I was feeling like a victim. I was arrogant and angry about my teammate's lack of production. I beat Dad home, showered, grabbed my usual bowl of post-game cereal, and watched some college hoops in the living room while I waited for him to get there. We usually didn't talk about basketball much after the game, but that night I wanted to complain. He always stayed true to his original plan about not bringing up our basketball team at home, but he'd talk to me about it if I approached him. At home, he was more like a trusted adviser than a coach. He walked in the door and sat down in his favorite recliner.

"Oh man. Guess we won't go undefeated," he said, tongue-in-cheek as he kicked off his shoes.

"Yep," I responded.

"Good job tonight. You shot the ball well," he said.

"Thanks, Dad," I said, but in my mind I was thinking, *Shot the ball well? I freakin' dropped 29 in a half. I was great.*

"Dad, what else can I do?" I asked, thinking the question would be rhetorical, but this wasn't actually a question. It was a thinly veiled brag.

Dad took a deep breath and said, "You know Josh, your teammates are good players. They've proven that. You're gonna have to trust them and get them more involved. It's hard for them to get into a rhythm when you are out there playing one on one and scoring 35 points, no matter how efficiently you are shooting the ball. Also, nobody plays defense as well when they are not involved at all in the offense. That's just how the game works. You tried to be a hero tonight, but in basketball there is no need for heroics on a good team. If you have to be a hero, you aren't playing on a very good team. Just remember that, but I'm proud of how hard you played. You have an amazing will to win, and I love it."

"Gotcha. Thanks Dad."

I was floored. I didn't know what to say. I liked

scoring in the mid to high thirties. It was fun. I was also a little hurt that Dad didn't say I played great, but Dad wasn't blinded by my great shooting performance. He knew I could run the team better. I had approached him, and he would never shy away from keeping it real when I asked for advice. I'm sure he knew that if I was averaging 30 points per game for the rest of the season, I would probably have a good chance to get a college scholarship in spite of my size. But that would never trump his desire for me to be a great teammate and make everyone I played with better. My career would never take precedence over our team being the best we could be. He gave me exactly what I needed in the moment. I needed to get over myself, stop trying to blame someone else, take personal responsibility, and think of ways to make the team better. He was proud of me for trying the best I knew how, but he couldn't pass up this teaching moment.

We picked up two more convincing wins the week following the Boyd game and had climbed to #2 in the TSSAA AP poll. We weren't fat and satisfied, but we were starting to think we were good. Dad definitely had some hard coaching to do to get us ready for post season play. V, Joel, Caleb, and I crashed at Eric's house on a Friday night after we laid a vicious homecoming beat down on Charleston High School. The next week we would have three games. We never practiced on Sundays, so Dad scheduled practice on Saturday morning. Of course, the five of us stayed up half the night and came into practice sluggish. Dad noticed it early in the practice and just sent us all packing like he did the year before. We hadn't had a poor practice all year. We had set the bar high for ourselves, and Dad would keep us accountable. We got the message.

The next Monday, I was still having a hard time letting Dad's lesson after the Boyd loss sink in, because of my pride and immaturity. During practice, my heroic selfishness rose to the surface again. Lance Walters fouled me hard on a driving layup during a mini-game toward the end of practice. I am not sure why I took exception to the foul. Maybe it was a temporary bout with entitlement, or maybe I had a flashback of my sophomore year when I broke my ankle on a foul by his brother. Regardless of the reasoning, I made it my personal mission to abuse him every possession for the rest of practice. I would put the heat on him on the next defensive possession, stripping him of the ball and taking it in for a layup. The next 3 possessions I went at him hard on offense. It became a one on one battle while my teammates watched. Dad could see what was going on. He knew me better than anyone in the world, and he didn't do personal missions. V knocked the ball off of Eric's leg out of bounds near where Dad was standing on the sideline. It would be our ball on the side. Before V could inbound the ball to me, Dad stepped out onto the floor behind me. I felt a hard yank on the back of my practice jersey. I took a step back as he started speaking to me in a quiet voice.

"Hey Superman, how 'bout you quit trying to be the hero again. You know how that works out for us."

I was seething, but I think his point was finally starting to sink in. Maybe I just needed to hear it again.

He coached us hard, but we trusted him. We actually embraced it. He would always say, "If I'm not coaching you hard, I probably don't think you have it in you." When he got after us, sometimes our blood pressure would rise with his, but we wouldn't sulk around with hurt feelings. Even if we were angry, we knew that his hard coaching was complimentary at its core, and we would raise our intensity level and rise to the occasion.

Dad doing what he does best- teaching the game.

Lefty locked in

41

OUR TEAM LOST SOME tough games against Lookout Valley, Boyd, and CCS during second semester, but we ended the regular season playing good ball and carried a 20-4 record into tournament time. We would host the District 5A tournament at Vance Gym.

After thrashing Grace in the District semifinal, we would face this year's nemesis, Boyd Buchanan, who had swept us during the regular season. Dad had us as prepared as we ever were. The house was filled to capacity and people started to get turned away by the fire marshal by the 5-minute mark of warm ups. Our crowd was always huge for such a small school. It helped that there was a University next door who loved good basketball, and a church on campus that had over 2,000 members. So fans came to watch our games in droves. Every game (even road games) during the announcement of our starting lineup, most of our students and some recent alumni would come out of the stands and onto the court to form a tunnel at the end of our mini starting lineup tunnel of players. Dad called it 'The Posse.' Most of the time it would extend to the sideline across our bench and open up around half court, where we would pop out to shake hands with the opposing coach, but 'The Posse' was out of control this night. They extended the tunnel past half court to the opposite corner where it turned in, opening up around the free throw line on the other side of the floor. It felt like it took five minutes to get through 'The Posse,' and I'm sure the opposing coaches in the district were having second thoughts about letting us host the District 5A tournament. It was quite an experience though, and thanks to our rowdy fans, it's safe to say that we had a significant home court advantage.

"The Posse" during starting lineups for the District 5A championship

In the first quarter, we jumped out to an early lead by shredding Boyd's three-quarter-court press. Caleb forced them to call off their press by knocking down 3 straight shots in the corner out of our press break offense. I was distributing the ball and getting my teammates easy buckets as well as I had all season.

With 20 seconds left in the third quarter, we were ahead 45-35 as I dribbled a few steps inside of half court. Our other four players went to the baseline to spread the floor. This play would allow me to read the defense if one of their men decided to help up or double me. Dad had prepared me for moments like these with drills to create space from my defender in practice. I would dribble hard at them and back dribble sharply to escape the five second count. Dribble around some more. Then do it again. Dad always said, "Get the shot off with 3 seconds left. That will give us time for an offensive rebound and score if you miss." Everyone in the gym knew I was taking the shot.

10...9...8... I back dribbled again, and glanced at Dad. He was sitting in his patented Coach T squat in front of the bench with a smirk on his face holding up 3 fingers in front of his chest.

You got it Dad, I thought.

6...5...4... I lowered my shoulder and drove right like I was about to take it to the rim. My defender backed off in retreat. I stopped on a dime from 23 feet out, rose up, and shot a quick release 3-point shot. Kill shot. We were up 13. They crowd was going wild. It gave me so much confidence knowing that Dad believed in me like that. The look on his face before I took the shot exuded confidence like he knew I would make it.

The kill shot with Dad looking on

We rocked them in front of our home crowd 63-46. I lead us with 21. Caleb, V, and Joel also scored in double figures. We would cut down our own nets and enter the region tournament after playing our best game of the season.

The region tournament would be played across the street at our home away from home, Tennessee Temple University's McGilvary Gym. After a sluggish start, we took care of business against South Pittsburg 65-53 in the first round. The tournament trail was set up different this year. The TSSAA was tinkering with the format. For the next three years, the sub-state game would be replaced with the sectional tournament. The sectional tournament would take the top 3 teams from the two neighboring regions to play a 6 team single elimination tournament with each region champ getting a bye in the first round. The top 2 teams in the sectional would advance to state. This meant that the all-important region semifinal game was no longer 'loser goes to the house.' There would be a consolation game between the two losers of the region semifinal to see who advanced to the sectionals. The TS-SAA decided to make our complicated tournament even more complicated for one reason... money.

Regardless, the region semifinals were still important. Nobody wanted to play in the 'do or die' consolation elimination game. McGilvary gym was packed for the semifinal showdown between 'The Big 4' in Region 2A. Lookout Valley beat Boyd 55-43, and we jumped all over CCS early and held on for a 66-61 win avenging our two regular season losses to them.

CCS ended Boyd's season in the region consolation game, and the region championship would be a grudge match between long-time rivals Temple and Lookout Valley. I always seemed to play well offensively against Valley. Both games we played against Lookout Valley that year had been decided in overtime. I hit 9 threes and posted a career high 39 points in our overtime win at their place earlier in the season, and at our place I had another big game posting 27 points including a 35-footer at the end of regulation to send the game to overtime. Valley took that one though.

Valley guarded me very well in the first half running double teams at me when I came off screens and when I dribbled the ball across half court. They took an early lead and had a 9-point advantage at the half, but we wanted that elusive region championship banner and wouldn't go down without a fight. Midway through the fourth quarter, we were down 42-37. I made three consecutive buckets, and we got three straight stops to take a 43-42 lead. The last bit of the fourth quarter was a defensive war with neither team giving an inch. We found ourselves down 45-43 with 23 seconds left when I drove into the lane and dished it off to Joel for a layup that tied the game. On Valley's ensuing possession we were called for a foul. C.J. Taylor went to the line and drained both free throws, and we found ourselves down by 2 with 6 seconds left when Valley called timeout.

We sat down on the bench. All eyes were locked on Dad as he drew the first letters of our names where we would be on his white board.

"The ball will be in Josh's hands." He knew they couldn't keep me from getting it. "Valley is going to double him when he crosses half court. One of you is going to get this shot. Step up and take it with confidence. We all believe in you," he said. "Josh, make the read and the right basketball play. If they don't double you, knock one down."

Dad was a master strategist. He often knew what our opponents would do before it happened. We used to joke that he was basketball's Nostradamus. V was inbounding and I caught the ball on the run. Caleb and Jeron were in the corners, ready to fire a 3 for the win if their man helped. Joel was under the basket ready for a dish off layup. V would be following the play ready for a kick-back if his man got sucked in on my drive. It all played out as Dad planned. As I was flying across half court I saw Jeron's man start running toward me. I veered away from him as I crossed the 3-point line to try to get him sucked into the paint even more. I had already made the read. When I got a foot in the paint, I leaped and kicked it across the floor to a wide open Jeron, with seconds remaining. It looked good leaving his hand, but careened off the back of the rim as time expired. Lookout Valley won the Region 3A championship 47-45.

A rowdy Temple crowd at the Region Championship in McGilvary Gym

42

THE NEXT WEEK WE loaded up the bus and headed to the sectional tournament at Tennessee Tech University. We were confident and ready to make our run at a state championship. On the trip to Tech, I went up to the front of the bus and sat down with Dad. I knew I only had a few weeks at the most to play for him, and I wanted to spend some time with him on the way up.

"What's up, Josh? Not used to seeing you on this side of the bus." Dad said.

"Ah, nothing really. Just wanted to see what you thought about Celina." I inquired about the team we would be playing in the opening round. I actually just wanted to hang out.

"They're pretty big. Not DCA or McCallie big, but they are strong. Lotta football players," he replied.

"That should be good. Rather play big and strong than fast and skilled. We can always break big and strong," I said.

"Yep. Are you nervous?" he asked.

"No," I lied. I didn't want my high school basketball career to end. Just the thought of it was depressing. I also didn't have any scholarship offers on the table, which made me a little nervous too. I knew deep down I shouldn't worry about that, but I couldn't help myself. I desperately wanted to play basketball after high school. Basketball was all I knew. It was my identity.

"That's good. No need to be, but I'd understand if you were," he said. I think he knew I was a little nervous.

"Just remember, you don't have to shoot great for us to win, and you don't have to play great for me to be proud of you. You just have to be you. You pour your soul into this game and this team. I've never seen you take the floor in a game when you didn't give it everything you had. That's all you can do. Ain't it?"

"Ya... but I just wanna win so bad," I said.

"I know. We all do, but you get to compete. Don't forget that. Look back there."

I turned around and saw Higgs two rows behind us, head bobbing up and down, jamming out with his headphones on. He was definitely getting his game face on. I smiled.

"Higgs doesn't get to play. He never will. Just enjoy the moment and don't waste a second worrying. Cut loose. Have the time of your life, man. If you're grateful for simply getting to go out there and play, you won't have time to be nervous because you'll be totally in the moment," he said.

"You're right, Dad."

He continued, "I don't know anyone who loves to play more than you do. It's so much fun to watch."

I could've run through a brick wall in that moment. Only minutes before, that common senior year fear (the fear of it being over) was manifesting itself in my head. That fear that paralyzes so many seniors every year and keeps them from letting it all hang out. Fear that can turn a relentless warrior into a protective game manager who is holding something back. Not now. Dad knew what to say. He sensed it in the one sentence that I uttered, and his words empowered me to go out and play my best with no fear of failure.

We got off to a 9-0 start against Celina in the first round. They regrouped and cut our lead to 6 by half-time, but our speed eventually broke them and we went on to a 69-51 win.

We would square off against the Region 4A champs, the Upperman Bees, in the Sectional Semifinal. This was the new 'do or die' game. Winner advances to the finals and punches their ticket to the state tournament in Murfreesboro. Loser gets housed. The Bees were led by a dynamic three guard attack. They had speed on the perimeter and size in the paint, but we were confident and playing great basketball. My teammates had been stepping up big time. V and Joel were playing the best ball of their careers, and Caleb had been a shot making assassin all year long. He had really turned it on down the home stretch.

The game was played at a frenetic pace from the opening tip. Both teams were used to bringing the heat on defense, but the guard play of both teams was too strong to break. We shredded each other's full-court pressure resulting in easy buckets at both ends during the first quarter. We backed off the pressure in the second quarter and placed our focus on getting stops. Upperman kept trying to press us, and we kept slicing and dicing. I had a monster first half scoring 18 points by playing with the liberating looseness that Dad was talking about on the bus. We took a 32-25 lead into halftime.

The Bees kept chipping away at our lead in the second half, inching their way back without making any big runs. They finally took their first lead of the game when guard Nick Davis hit two free throws with 58.5 seconds left. After an empty possession at our end, we were down by 2 and forced to foul Davis again with 24 seconds left. He hit the front end of the one and one and missed the second. With us trailing 56-53, Joel grabbed the rebound. We calmly brought it down the floor and ran an old faithful set that would bring me off of a staggered double screen to get a 3-point shot at the top of the key. I got a great look thanks to solid screens by Joel and V, but the ball grazed the front rim just enough to rim out off the back rim.

I had a split-second flashback to my miss at the end of regulation in the state championship last year. That shot haunted me the entire summer, and I used it as motivation. I worked hard to make sure that if I had another chance to hit a championship shot, I would be prepared. I may not hit it, but I'll want it and fully expect to make it because I had done the work. During my senior season I had made five 3 point shots in the final 8 seconds of games that either won the game or sent it to overtime.

I was shocked. I had missed the game winner again.

But wait... we were still in it because I still had brothers who were fighting for our basketball lives. Joel slapped the ball away from Upperman's big man as he tried to secure the rebound. As the ball rolled across the lane, V dove (Dennis Rodman style) to grab it. A swarm of Bees quickly surrounded him on the floor, and a dog pile ensued. The officials blew their whistles and called a jump ball with 3.2 seconds left. We had the possession arrow and got the ball under our basket. Dad called timeout as I breathed a sigh of relief knowing that we would get another shot.

Dad drew up his version of America's play. I would inbound it straight to Caleb who would be popping out just past the top of the key. Then I could run off either a single screen from Joel on one side or a double screen from Jeron and V on the other. I knew they would be switching whichever screen I came off, but I knew that I could get the shot off. Because I had quickened my release over the summer, all I needed was a slither of space.

As we were walking out of the huddle, Joel said, "Come my way. I'll get you open."

I believed him. He was the best screener I had ever played with. His screens were probably responsible for over half of the 90 threes I made that season. I nodded at Caleb and it was understood that I would be most likely going off of Joel's screen. The ref handed me the ball and began his count. I lobbed the ball to Caleb at the top as planned, faked toward V, and sprinted toward Joel who knocked my man to the floor with his screen. As expected, Joel's man switched off to try to cover me. I was in a full sprint toward the arc, and Caleb delivered a perfect pass to my shooting pocket. I caught the ball and rose up to try to get a quick-release shot off over the long reach of Upperman's big man. The ball flew right over his fingertips as he landed on top of me. We were both on the floor and I couldn't see a thing. I just heard our crowd erupt as the horn sounded. It was nothing but nylon. I couldn't believe it and felt a sweet redemption. Joel ran over to me and picked me up off the floor. It was a lucky shot, but as the Roman philosopher Seneca said, "Luck is what happens when preparation meets opportunity." All I could do was point to the good Lord and slap Joel on the chest. He made the play with his screen. When we got to the bench, I was sure we would not be denied in the overtime period.

The Bees had other plans. Those guys were tough too. They hit a layup on the opening tip, but V countered with a driving layup. V fouled out on the Bee's next possession. They made both free throws, and I missed a fifteen foot pull up in the lane on our ensuing possession. We were behind the eight ball with three minutes left when Upperman went into their delay offense to try to force us to foul them. We brought intense pressure, but we couldn't shake them up and were forced to foul. Upperman went 4-6 from the line down the stretch and held on to win 67-62.

My high school career was over. I had to fight to

hold back the tears while we shook hands with the Bees. They had matched our will and toughness. I had a lot of respect for them and wished them the best in the state tournament. When I went into the locker room the first person I saw was Higgs. He was standing in one of the corners sobbing. I remembered standing in a similar corner waiting on Karl Lewis to enter the locker room 6 years before. I went straight to him and hugged his neck, and we cried together.

Higgs struggled to get out words, "I'm so p-p-proud to be your brother, Josh."

I grabbed him by the sides of his face and said with my voice choking up, "No. Mitch. I'm proud to be your brother. You inspire me more than you'll ever know. Thank you."

Then Dad walked in. We all stood silent waiting for him to say the first word.

His eyes filled with tears as he tried to collect his thoughts and his composure. "I love you guys, and I'm going to miss coaching you seniors. You are all like sons to me, but I'm especially going to miss coaching you, Josh."

I couldn't believe he said that. He rarely said anything good about me in front of the guys, but what did it matter at this point. I was done. He wasn't worried about favorites. He let everyone know right then and there that I was his favorite. I was his son. His words meant so much to me. I walked toward him with tears streaming down my face and my jersey still soaked in sweat, and gave him the biggest bear hug I had given him since I was ten. I didn't want it to be over. I didn't want to let go. When I finally did, his shirt was soaked in my sweat and our tears, and he had the image of my jersey imprinted across his chest.

TEMPLE

3

43

OUR SEASON ENDED WITH a 25-7 record. I averaged 24 points, 6 assists and 4 steals per game during my senior campaign, and was selected as one of three finalists for the Mr. Basketball award in Class A, as well as first team All-State. I was getting a lot of attention from the Associated Press and the TSSAA, but I wasn't getting much attention from colleges. David Lipscomb University had shown a lot of interest early in the year, but they had backed off. Don Meyer had stepped down as head coach, and they decided to go Division 1. Unfortunately, Division 1 programs didn't have much use for a 5'9" 140-pound point guard. I had some interest from small schools around the area, but only one real offer on the table. That offer was from Rick Johnson across the street at Tennessee Temple University. I wasn't sure how much he really wanted me though, and I was pretty sure that he was getting a lot of pressure from the administration to sign me. I know he was concerned about my lack of size. Honestly, I didn't care if he believed in me or not. I just wanted to play. Proving I could play and earning my keep was standard for me.

Dad once told me, "If you're 5'9" you have to prove every day that you can play, and even if you do, colleges might not offer you. If you're a 6'5" guard you have to prove that you can't, and even if you prove you can't, someone will probably still offer you. It's just how it is. No point worrying about something you can't control. Just get as good as you possibly can and prove it every day."

When we got back to school, I was a little lost. I was uncertain about the future and was still grieving from our heartbreaking defeat in the sectionals. I couldn't pay attention in class and just floated through school like a shell of myself for the first few days. On Wednesday the next week I went to put books in my locker after school and saw an envelope taped to it with the letters 'J.T.' on it. I could tell it was one of Dad's patented hand-written letters. I went home, sat on my bed, and opened my letter.

Tennessee Temple Academy

Kindergarten and Nursery
School - Ages 2-5
493-4265

Elementary School
Grades 1-6
493-4211

High School
Grades 7-12
493-4337

Josh,

Well it is all over. I'm so proud of you. You did great all year long. You cared more about the team than yourself. You gave it all every practice + every game. No scoreboard could make you a loser.

You'll never know how much joy you have given me thru the years. The pride I have for you + the love I feel cannot be put in words. That has nothing to do with basketball + everything to do with character, self-respect and integrity. That's what makes a man — nothing else matters.

On the basketball side of things thanks for making this a year to remember. We showed the state what a team can do + it was awesome. I'm sorry for all you put up with being the coaches' kid - you handle it really well. Don't O.D. on basketball - take care of those that care about you.

You're the best,
Dad.

1907 Bailey Avenue • Chattanooga, Tennessee • 37404

Little did we know, we were about to do it all again.

PART 3

THE COLLEGE YEARS

44

I N EARLY APRIL, I signed a letter of intent to play for Rick Johnson at Tennessee Temple University. I was excited about the opportunity, but I was also relieved. I really liked Coach Johnson's coaching style, and it would be nice to play out my college career in my hometown where everyone could come to my games. T.T.U. had a long tradition of excellence. After Lefty and Ron Bishop won their four NCCAA national championships. Tim Collins—my old shooting coach— had led his team to two more national championships. After Collins left, the program went through some tough times, but Coach Johnson had put them back on the national map by winning 99 games in the last four seasons. It was an honor for me to be a part of his program. I always bled red and white anyway.

However, shortly after I signed, Coach Johnson stepped down. It was an uneasy feeling not knowing who the coach would be after you had just signed scholarship papers, but that feeling would be gone soon.

The administration wasted no time contacting Dad to ask him to consider moving up to the college. He told me when they asked him, and I was obviously ecstatic. I think he was pretty excited too. He was an alum who was in school when Lefty and Ron were hanging banners in the rafters. He loved T.T.U., so it didn't take him long to jump at the opportunity to be a college head coach at his alma mater. It was hard to believe I would get the opportunity to play for him for 4 more years, but I had a lot of work to do to get my body ready for the speed and strength of the college game.

T.T.U. had graduated a talented senior class. I knew that if I worked hard and gained a little weight, I could earn a good deal of playing time as a freshman. I was still getting up my 600 shots per day and playing a ton of ball. Gaining weight was the big challenge for me. I tried everything to fatten myself up. I ate a peanut butter and jelly sandwich with every meal. I lifted weights, took creatine supplements, and drank protein shakes. Nothing seemed to work. My frame just wasn't meant to be that big. It probably didn't help that I burned calories daily like a rapper burns money. By the first day of school I had gained a whopping 7 pounds.

College was an exciting time. Tennessee Temple University was tiny by most college standards, but to me it was huge. There were over 300 incoming freshmen. My graduating class in high school had 25 students. Our high school was so small you could walk into the bathroom and tell who was sitting on the john by seeing their shoes under the stall. There were so many new people to meet. I was a social butterfly though, so this seemed like heaven.

Our team was young. We had two seniors. Point guard Ryan Alexander and guard Scott Weldy. Ryan had a great freshman year. He showed a lot of promise, but chronic back injuries would haunt him throughout his career. He was still solid, but by the time he was a senior he was a shell of his former self. Weldy was a glue guy. He was tough and could run all day. His will and skill set would fit perfectly into Dad's defensive oriented system.

Our guy was 6'2" junior Steve Robison. Steve is the best player I ever played with. He was coming off an All-American season the year before. He was the college version of Gabe (too big for the guards to handle and too fast for the bigs). A guy who can score at will is a point guards dream. Just get the ball to Steve in a scoring position on the floor, and he'll do the rest. Our sophomores were 6'6" enforcer Rob Moore, and 6'3" lights-out shooter Aaron Young.

Our incoming freshman class would be heavily relied on during the course of the season. 6'5" Craig Price was our best post scorer. He had an array of moves over either shoulder in the post, and could also stretch opposing defenses with his 3-point shooting. He was a small college Kevin Love. I saw him play at the Murphy Center in the AA state tournament against Chattanooga power Brainerd High School in '98, and couldn't wait to play with him. Joining Craig inside was 6'8" Mirek Holan and 6'6" Blake Kirby. Both were athletic and would add depth to our inside attack. 6'5" forward Nathan Ranew and 6'2" shooting guard Andre Dubois would take redshirt years to get acclimated to the college game. Then there was 5'10" explosive guard Brad Green. Brad was a blue blood from Louisville, Kentucky. He was a good shooter and could electrify the crowd with his amazing dunking ability. The only thing more explosive than his game was his personality. We hit it off during freshman orientation, and I had a new running mate.

The college game was a big adjustment for me physically. Preseason practice seemed so long. We started lifting and playing pick-up together as a team in August, and actually started practice in mid-September. Our first game wasn't until November 1st, so we would have six weeks of practice under our belt before we ever donned the uniform. It was taxing on my body. No longer would I be competing against the 15 and 16-year-old boys on our high schools second team. I would be competing against grown men who were of legal drinking age and outweighed me by at least 30 pounds. Now, I was the boy.

As is the case with most freshman seasons, mine was the most polarized season of my career. It was filled with incredible highs and vicious lows. I had a great preseason and earned a valuable role in the team as our first guard off the bench.

Our first game would be against NAIA preseason #6 ranked Lambuth University. I had been dealing with a nagging hip flexor issue, so I made my way to the training room to get some treatment before the game. When I walked in I couldn't believe my eyes. There sat 7'1" Sibu Mabaso getting his ankle taped on one of the tables. He was sitting down and was still almost a head taller than me, and I'm certain that he was double my weight. *Looks like we won't be getting much around the rim tonight,* I thought to myself.

I don't remember much from the game because it seemed so fast. The speed was night and day compared to high school. Our student section—known as 'The Crazies'—was wild that night. I do remember receiving a proper welcome to college basketball from Lambuth's point guard. He was a stocky senior who was as fast as he was physical. Not even a minute after I had checked into the game, I drove into the lane. He took an angle in front of me and hit me with a body stop. Hitting him was like hitting a brick wall. I fell to the ground and looked at the ref as if to say, *'Where's the foul?'* Without skipping a beat, Lambuth picked up the ball and headed down to the other end—leaving me in the dust. Nice first play of your career, huh? The good news was there was nowhere to go from there but up.

The game was tight the entire way. Lambuth was incredibly talented. Their roster was loaded with Division 1 transfers, and our team was playing way over our heads. Things looked pretty grim when we found ourselves down by 4 points with 6.4 seconds on the clock. Their point guard went to the line to shoot a double bonus. He made the first. Dad called timeout.

Dad drew up our sideline fast break to get us a quick shot. Lambuth's point guard missed the free-throw and Rob snatched the rebound. He turned and threw it to Steve streaking up the sideline. Steve caught it and fired a pass to me in the corner without taking a dribble. I caught it and shot a three that swished through the net with 1.8 seconds left the clock. We were down by 2. Dad called our last time out to set our press for one final attempt at a quick steal and score.

Lambuth couldn't get the ball inbounds. They called their last timeout. Let's try this again.

The second inbound attempt was more of the same. The inbounder started to panic as the ref's count approached five seconds. He launched the ball to half-court. Aaron Young intercepted the pass, took one dribble, and fired a 40-footer. Bang! What a way for Dad and I to start our college basketball careers! After that game, I started to think that we had something special brewing again at Temple.

45

WE FOLLOWED THAT GAME with a victory over Reinhardt College, but the next three games were not so kind, as we lost all three by an average of 4 points.

After that, our next game was on the road against long-time arch rival Lee University. Lee had a new coach as well, and both teams were young. I had been to many Temple/Lee games in my life, and the atmosphere was always nuts. Packed gyms, raucous student sections, bad blood, and highly competitive games were the standard when these two teams met. Temple/Lee was the Duke/UNC of small college basketball. The pageantry... the passion... the rivalry.

I remember one story from the early 90's. Lee used to always bring this massive white flag with maroon 'L' embroidered on it. During timeouts, a student would run the flag around the gym. They would always slow down to wave it right in front of the Temple student section. Tempers would flare. A few obscenities would be exchanged, but nothing more than that. Until one hotly contested battle at the McGilvary Gym in the mid-90's.

The Lee rowdies were about to take off and run with the flag during half time. A seemingly excited Lee student (decked out in a Lee Flames T-shirt and hat) asked the usual flag runners if he could have a go. They obliged. He took the flag and darted as fast as he could in front of the Lee student body. Their crowd erupted. He turned the corner and made his way to the Temple side, who greeted him with a chorus of boos. When he got to the front and center of the T.T.U. fans, he stopped. The boos got louder. He looked at the flag. Then he looked at the fans. He looked at the flag again, turned it upside down, and started mopping the floor with it! He was a Temple wolf in Lee clothing. The 'boos' quickly turned to cheers as a handful of Lee students emptied out of the stands to retrieve their stolen flag. Of course they were met by a host of Temple 'Crazies' coming to the defense of their new hero. The extra-curricular activities came to a head right in the middle of the floor. Punches were thrown, a few students were arrested, and the scene could best be described as pandemonium. It was safe to say there was never any love lost between the two schools.

Playing in Lee's Paul Dana Walker was a rush. It seated a little over 2,500 fans, and when Temple came to town there was not a seat to be had. I was too young and naive to fully understand how big this game was to both schools. I didn't think about the gravity of the moment and was just excited to play in the electric atmosphere and came off the bench firing. I hit six 3's and scored 22 points as we went on to win 84-78.

My first college season had gotten off to a great start as far as shooting the basketball was concerned. I was leading us in assists and was our second leading scorer in my role off the bench first semester, but things would soon change. My 145-pound wiry frame took a beating every game. Shortly after the Christmas break, my body began to break down, and as a result, my hot shooting wasn't sustainable. For a jump shooter, when the legs start to go, the shot falls apart from the ground up. My shots started coming up short on a consistent basis. Our team lost five of six games to drop to 10-17. I was struggling… and searching. Losing was new to me, and I didn't know how to handle it.

For only the second time in my life, my confidence was shaken, and I was beginning to doubt myself. The funny thing about self-doubt is that a magnified need for validation follows right behind.

One night before I went to bed, I went downstairs to talk to Dad. That night I had an agenda. I had developed a need for validation over this stretch of poor shooting and had lost sight of what mattered. I acted like I was going down to talk to him because I wanted to win, but in reality, I wanted something for myself—an ego boost. I wanted to start.

"Dad, we're struggling. I'm struggling. I'm not used to losing."

"We'll get through it. We're a young team. We have to stick together and just keep getting better," he replied.

"We might play better if I was starting," I said. I stood frozen in place. The words just came out. This is not how I had planned to start this conversation. Did I really just say that?

He cocked his head. "Is that what you're worried about? Starting? Seriously?"

I looked at the floor. "I play most of the minutes at the point. Why wouldn't I start?" I said. I was entering all new territory—I had never questioned him before—but my ego was overpowering my sense.

"There are many reasons, but I'm only going to give you one. Because I want you to trust me," he said.

"This team NEEDS the punch you bring off the bench," he continued. "You gotta trust me. Have I earned your trust?"

"Yes, but—" He stopped me there. I wanted to continue telling him how the best players should be starting. I'm glad he didn't let me... I would have dug a deeper hole that would have caused him to trust me less. I knew better. I just let my temporary insecurities get the best of me. I needed to just shut up and listen.

"Josh, I'm gonna stop you right here. This is how it is. Get over yourself. Just get better every day, play hard, and be you. This isn't you. I don't know this guy who worries about starting. The guy I've always known only cares about the team, trusts the coaching staff, coaches on the floor and is a great teammate. Just work hard every day and let the chips fall where they may. Do you really need validation or accolades? You're worrying about what doesn't matter. Get your focus right and be you again."

"Yessir," I said, walking dejectedly up the stairs. I thought about it all night. *Who do I think I am?* He reminded me. As always, I knew he was right. I was humbled and ashamed. But tomorrow was a chance to turn it all around, and I wouldn't miss that chance.

I practiced with a new sense of purpose and joy the next day. I didn't care about making or missing shots.

I was gonna run the show. No longer would I be stuck inside myself. I was gonna be the guy who makes his teammates better and get back to being a real point guard. Steve exploded down the stretch of the season, and I made sure he got the rock early and often.

We finished that season winning 8 of our last 9 games. We won the NCCAA South Region Tournament and made it to the National Tournament where we lost an overtime heartbreaker to Bartlesville Wesleyan. Steve scored nearly 1000 points in that season alone. He averaged 27 points and 6 rebounds per game, and I finished the year averaging 10 points and 5.5 assists per game.

46

I WOULD ADD TWO major things to my game that summer. First, I committed to changing my body. I would always be small. There was nothing I could do about that, but I never wanted to feel small again. Dad's assistant coach, Jody Bailey, came up with a personal plan for me to gain weight and strength, so my teammate Aaron Young and I lived in the weight room.

Secondly, I had to get my 3-point shot off even quicker for the college game. Jody also helped me clean up my footwork which allowed my shot to be even quicker. I cut all the fat off the bone of my shot. Every motion was minimal and efficient, and the strong foundation of my shot made me even more consistent. Jody Bailey was the latest in the long list of specialists that would help me take my game to new heights, and I'm thankful that Dad hired him at T.T.U.

My new running mate Brad Green didn't really care for school too much. He had a good season in basketball, but decided that college was not for him and left at the end of the year. I hated to see him go.

By the time my sophomore season was under way, I had gained 20 pounds. I weighed 165 pounds and was bench pressing 265. Brad, Mirek, and Blake left the program, but we had four good players transfer in. 5'8" point guard Drew Murphy returned to the program. He was the starting point guard at Temple during Rick Johnson's final year at the helm, but had transferred to Rhodes College to be closer to home when Coach Johnson left Temple. I guess he wanted to play with his boys Steve and Rob again. I was pumped about him coming back. I played a lot of pick-up with Drew when I was in high school. He was a good guy and a great competitor.

A lot of college players feel threatened when their coach recruits a good player who plays the same position as them. This is the result of a lack of confidence. When you are confident, you want the best players possible to come in to your program. You want to be on a great team. In college, that means all the good players with good character that you can find. I was as confident as I had ever been in my career, because I had put in the work. I looked forward to joining forces with Drew and competing with him at practice. We knew we would make each other better.

Craig's old high school teammate, 6'2" sophomore Travis Williams signed as well. Travis was an amazing talent who transferred in after a good freshman season at NCAA Division 2 Carson Newman University in Knoxville. He came to Temple because he wanted to have a career in the ministry. The final two pieces to the puzzle were junior transfers 6'4" swingman Quincy Young and 6'5" forward Scott McDonald. Both could play inside and on the perimeter.

My personal favorite newcomer was my old teammate David "V" Casteel. V walked on that year. Dad always had a special place on every team he coached for an energy guy that loved to get dirty, and V was that guy to the max. In games, if the team was struggling and needed a shot in the arm, Dad would send V to the scorer's table. V never missed an opportunity to dive for a loose ball or draw a charge. For our team, he was a pair of jumper cables. I'm not sure if they tracked it, but if they did, I know beyond a shadow of a doubt that V set the Temple's all-time records for charges drawn, floor burns, and fouls per minute. He was amazing.

We got off to a good start and had a 10-5 record at the break. We continued to play well second semester and had posted a seven game winning streak heading into the Paul Dana Walker Arena to play Lee. They had their most talented team in the long history of the school. Led by UMass transfer Jovann Johnson, they beat us for the second time that year in a game that went right down to the wire. After the Lee loss, we rebounded and won five straight.

I was playing great. My new body was coming through in the clutch. I was averaging 12.5 points and 7 assists per game while shooting over 40% from beyond the arc. We were 20-10 poised to make a deep tournament run, but at practice before we would go on the road to play Birmingham Southern, Dad and I would butt heads.

I had played for Dad for so long that we usually knew what the other was thinking. Often times, we could communicate with nothing more than a look. There were times when we both took this for granted. Toward the end of practice, we were playing mini games. Dad was coaching the first team, and Lefty and Jody were coaching the second team. The score was tied with 3 seconds on the clock. We were inbounding and had to go the full length of the floor for a game winning shot attempt. Dad liked to experiment with new plays sometimes at the end of these mini games. He told Steve to go one way and me to go another. I seriously had no idea what he wanted me to do. As we walked to our spots on the floor, I looked at

Steve. He shrugged his shoulders as if to say, *I don't know either.* Jody handed Craig the ball for the inbounds pass. Steve zigged. I zagged. Craig launched a full court pass to no one. It bounced once and hit the bleachers behind the goal on the opposite end.

Dad yelled from across the floor, "Josh, what are you doing? Do you need me to draw you a map?"

"That'd be nice!" I fired back at the top of my lungs.

My sarcastic tone took everyone by surprise. You could hear a pin drop as my words echoed across the gym. Dad walked toward me on the other side of the floor. It felt like it took an hour for him to get there. I knew what I had coming. It didn't matter whose fault the miscommunication was. I had disrespected him in front of the team for the first time in my 20 years on the earth.

He got inches from my face. No one but me could hear a word he was saying. I don't remember what he said exactly because I was so pissed. It was something to the effect of, you better never, ever disrespect me again. He sent me to the locker room, and my day would end there. As I made my exit he was locked on my shoulder whispering sweet nothings into my ear. Okay, there was nothing sweet about what he was saying. I sat in my locker and started packing my gear when Lefty walked in. Lefty was like my second father. Like Dad, if his mouth was moving, I was listening.

"You have been playing for your Dad a long time, man," Lefty said. "This was bound to happen sooner or later. I'm kinda surprised it took this long."

"I'm sick of it. Everything is different for me," I said. "I just want to be a regular player on the team."

"No. You don't," Lefty shot back. "Nothing about you has ever wanted regular."

"Ya. I'll give you that," I said.

"You're good, which means he's gonna be harder on you. You're tough, which means he's gonna be harder on you. You're his son, which means he's gonna be harder on you. That's how it is. I figured by now you'd be used to it," he said.

"Ya well it gets old. And all that doesn't make it right."

"No it doesn't, but do you need him to be easy on you? Is that what you need? Easy?" he asked, already knowing the answer.

"No," I said, as I stared at the floor.

"Well, I don't care who messed up the play. You were wrong for your disrespect. You know that, so make it right," he said.

"You're right. I will," I said.

"Ya'll will be just fine, man," he said, as he walked out.

I didn't get in my car to go home. I waited in his office until practice was over. When he came in I apologized for being disrespectful, he chewed me out again, and we moved on.

We were 21-11 heading into the finals of the South Region Tournament. We would face our most daunting challenge of the year. Gardner Webb University was in transition from NCAA Division 2 to Division 1. They had to sit out of Atlantic Sun Conference post season play for two years, so they would compete in the NCCAA tournament. If we were going to win the tournament, we would have to do it against a Division 1 opponent.

Gardner Webb built an early lead, but we stormed back. We were down 4 with 2 minutes to play. They made their free throws in the final minutes, and held on for a 78-72 victory. I scored 25 points and played my best game of the year against the best team we had faced, but I was heartbroken. This team was capable of so much more, and we all knew it. We played hard. The ball just didn't bounce our way, and our season ended right there.

Steve throws down a dunk vs. Lee

47

BEFORE FINAL EXAMS AT the end of my sophomore year, I got sick, real sick. One night I was trying to finish a term paper that I had procrastinated on, and I couldn't write. The words jumped all over the page, and my head was spinning. I started sleeping 20+ hours per day, and didn't know what was wrong with me. It was like my brain was just floating in a dream-like state during my waking hours. I was stuck in a nightmare. On a Wednesday night, Rachael came home from church to find me unconscious, lying face down on the living room floor. She didn't know what to do and couldn't get ahold of Mom or Dad, so she rushed me to the hospital. For the next three days, the doctors ran tests to try to figure out what was wrong with me. Brain scans, MRI's, a spinal tap... I received every neurological test in the book.

I don't remember much about my hospital stay, besides the spinal tap. That was pretty unforgettable. The only other thing I remember was the doctor coming to give Mom and Dad an update. I had my eyes half open drifting in and out of consciousness.

I heard the doctor tell my parents, "I think we have narrowed it down to three possibilities. Multiple Sclerosis, Viral Encephalitis, or a Brain Tumor."

Dad held Mom as she began to weep. I can't imagine how my parents felt. They had already been through so much with Higgs, especially early on. Now this?

A tear ran down my cheek. *I'm dead,* I thought, as I drifted off to sleep.

I knew M.S. wasn't something I wanted to face. That would change my life forever. Viral encephalitis didn't sound good either. V's Aunt had caught the disease from a mosquito, and she passed away within three months. I didn't even want to think about a brain tumor. My brain scans showed that I had a pinky fingernail sized spot right in the middle of my brain. The doctors said it could have been some sort of cyst or benign tumor that I'd had my entire life. But, if it was malignant, I was in trouble. Because of the location, it was inoperable.

I had my life perfectly planned out up to this point, but the unexpected can happen at any time. Life had thrown me a curveball. Now, the question was… would it break into the strike zone so I could take a swing? Or would it hang high and hit me square in the head? Either way, I would have to adjust to whatever life threw at me.

Basketball didn't seem as important while I was laying in that hospital bed. For all I knew, I was on my death bed. What had I done with my life? What did I believe in? How much of what life had to offer did I actually experience? Who was I besides just a basketball player? I was so afraid of dying, and felt like I had so much more life to live. Thankfully, I would have more living to do.

A week passed. I was feeling better every day. I was awake more and felt like I could focus in short spurts. Everyone was praying—the high school, the university, the church, and countless other family friends from all over the country. All the prayers had been answered when the doctor came in with some good news. They ruled out those three conditions and were pretty confident that I had contracted Lyme disease, and it had run its course. I made a full recovery and had a new lease on life. With two more years to play basketball, I wanted to make the most of it, but I wanted to live my life, too.

When you feel like you might die, you start to see things differently. I had obsessed over basketball my entire life. I wanted to change, but I didn't know how.

That summer, I made few more adjustments to my game. Steve had graduated, so I knew Aaron Young and I would be called upon to pick up much of the scoring load. Physically, I worked mostly on my legs and my explosion. In my shooting workouts, I extended my range, worked on my first step explosion, and enhanced my ability to create my own shot. I felt like I was ready for a breakout season.

When the school year began, I started dating a girl named Abbie Langhorne. She was a beautiful Korean-American who I had noticed during our freshman year. I was just too obsessed with basketball to want a girlfriend at the time. But, now I was different. I wanted to live my life, so I asked her out. She was incredible, and I was completely blown away with how much I liked her. Every minute I spent with her was golden. In a short time, she had become my closest friend and confidant. With her, I felt more balance in my life.

My old buddy Brad Green moved back to town. He rented a small house at the foot of Lookout Mountain, and his place became our stomping ground for the rest of the year. I was enjoying hanging out with Abbie, V, Brad, and our other friends. For the moment, basketball wasn't everything to me. But unfortunately, that moment would pass, because I still had a lot to learn.

48

OUR TEAM HAD EXPERIENCE, BUT life without Steve would mean we would all have to adjust our roles. Our regular rotation had four seniors and four juniors. We opened the season with a 47-point waxing of Carver College out of Atlanta. Then we would travel to the familiar confines of the Murphy Center to play an exhibition game against Middle Tennessee State University. The Blue Raiders put their foot on the gas and raced out to an early lead. They wanted to crush the small school who almost tagged them two years ago, but we wouldn't go down quietly. We went on a 15-0 run in the second half to cut the lead to 6. But we dug ourselves too deep of a hole in the first half. They made their free throws in the final minute and won by 14.

I was playing and shooting well, and we had a

3-1 record heading to Paul Dana Walker to play our arch rivals. Lee had a strong team again and they were massive. I had been a thorn in their side for the last two years. It seemed I always had big games against them. Coach Rick Hughes was one of many coaches that we faced who adopted a game plan that included trying to rough me up. He would play two point guards (Frank Walker and Chuckie Campbell) who were not afraid to use their combined fouls in an attempt to throw me out of a rhythm and keep me from getting any easy shots.

Our team relied on my scoring, but Lee wouldn't make it easy. Every time I came off a screen, someone jumped out. If I came off a ball screen, I was double teamed. If I cut through the lane, a Lee Flame would greet me with elbows, shoulders, and hip checks. Campbell and Walker hand checked, held, and bumped me all over the floor. At times it was hard to move, but Coach Bailey had me physically ready for this challenge.

Just like every Temple/Lee game I had played in before, the atmosphere was palpable. The Rowdiest members of Lee's student section were in the end zone behind our first half basket. Their cheerleaders also stood in this baseline end zone. These girls were not your average cheerleaders. I'm fairly certain that most of them minored in player hating. Inbounding the ball on this baseline was a trip. They would only be a few feet from you, talking all sorts of smack, and the words that came out of their mouths were not for kids. Let's just say every time we played at Paul Dana Walker, my vocabulary grew exponentially, but not in a way that would make Mom happy.

I always carried myself with a certain swagger when I was on the court. If you're as little as I was AND you're the coach's son, you better have a few things going for you. First, you better have some talent. Second, you'd better have swagger and thick skin.

I wasn't always like that though. The thickening of my skin was definitely a process. When I started playing in college, I realized that the hecklers were on a whole different level. One of my favorite moments came during the first road game of my career at MTSU. Because the game was played during the Thanksgiving break, the Murphy Center was pretty empty. But their band was there, and they were bringing the heckling heat. When a big arena is empty, everything that is yelled out echoes. As we were coming out of a timeout, the gym was completely quiet.

The captain of the trash talking band yelled out, "Hey, number 3! This one's for you."

The band started playing the Huggies Pull-up Diaper song. He sang at the top of his lungs while they played, "I'm a big kid look what I can do. I can wear big kid pants too..."

I couldn't help but smile. That was clever. The best was when heckling fans would realize at some point in the game that I was the coach's kid. It was like a revelation that would give them new life and ammunition to reload their weapons of mass harassment. I always had an appreciation for clever hecklers. However, when I was younger and more insecure, the things they said did sting. But they were part of my basketball life, and I would learn to deal with them.

At first I hated when they called me 'daddy's boy.' As my career progressed and I started getting better, I began to enjoy it. They gave me extra motivation. Plus, dealing with them was like a game within the game. The fact that I was a little cocky made them come at me even harder. If I'm being completely honest, I was probably more than a little cocky. I didn't do a whole lot of trash talking, I let my game speak for itself. But I wasn't shy about rubbing salt in the wound when it was time for my hecklers to eat some crow. I got the 'daddy's boy' shtick so often that I actually started to feed off of it. There was nothing I loved more than sticking it right in their faces when I knocked down a big shot. I wanted them to come face to face with a simple fact—this little daddy's boy owned their basketball soul.

Back at Lee, we were playing well in the first half. I had gotten some good looks and made them pay. With 3 minutes left in the half, I was fouled by Campbell on a 3- point shot attempt, and would go to the line to shoot three.

I stepped to the line and started my normal free throw routine. One, two, three dribbles, deep breath. The 2,000 plus Lee fans who were trying to distract me with their noise turned dead silent in my head.

Release, rotation, short. How short? The ball didn't even graze the front rim. In the words of Marlon Brando in Apocalypse Now, "The horror."

As expected, the Lee fans went absolutely bonkers. "Airball... Airball... Airball." My head was spinning as this chorus rained down on me.

Whoops, I thought to myself, as I stepped to the line for my next attempt. The official tossed the ball back to me.

One, two, three dribbles. Deep breath. This time the noise did not turn to silence in my head. Release, rotation, long. How Long? I was going to make sure I didn't leave this one short. I over corrected, and the ball made contact on the flat part of the back of the rim and the backboard. It was an ugly miss. The Lee fans were still chanting, "Airball." I stepped into the lane to exchange fives with Craig and Rob in an attempt to distract myself from the two most aesthetically unpleasant misses of my career.

When I went through my routine the third time, my head was filled with noise. The volume was paralyzing. My third shot felt good on the release, but it bounced off the back of the rim. I had just missed three straight free throws. That was a first. I was an 80+% free throw shooter for my career. It was in my head for the rest of the game. Every time I caught the ball the relentless Lee crowd would chant, "Airball."

The game was close until Lee broke away in the final minutes. The final score was 74-62, and I went 7-14 from the line.

I put the loss directly on my shoulders. For the first time in my career, I mentally wilted in the pressure packed atmosphere. All because of one stupid free throw. I was committed to not let this happen again. Every day I would get to practice early to get a shooting workout in. I would get up normal game speed shots for about 15 minutes. I would also get up 100 free throws before practice and 100 after. The more I shot, the more things seemed to get worse. I realized this was not a problem of preparation. This problem was in my head.

For the rest of the semester I took a trip through the shooting twilight zone. I shot a hair over 50% from the line and 30% from 3 for the whole semester. The worse things got the more everyone tried to help solve the problem, which only exacerbated it. Dad knew that the problem was mental, so he never once tried to help me correct my form. He never even acknowledged the problem of my shooting woes to me or to the team. He knew that the more I thought about it, the worse it would get. He only tried to help me change my focus. He coached me up on my overall game. He would kick me out of the gym after practice while I was getting up extra free throws. He would say, "Quit thinking about it. It's not helping." This was all new to me. I didn't know any other way to fix it but to get up more shots. I should have listened to his wisdom, but I wanted so badly to be great that I kept working. I knew our team needed me to step up in the scoring department, and I wanted to take control of my game and my shooting. I put more pressure on myself every day and was obsessed. My life was out of balance again, and it was a miserable experience.

During this period, Dad and I had the biggest blowup of my career. Dad had been going through a lot of stress too. He had just been diagnosed with diabetes, and his blood sugar levels were off the charts, constantly affecting his mood and his energy levels. It was the perfect storm for two stressed out people who had spent 8 years being around each other all the time.

At practice before our final home game of the semester we were doing the defensive shell drill. V and I had done this drill so many times during our career that we could do it in our sleep. V caught the ball on the wing. I was guarding him when Dad said, "Freeze." When he said that, everyone would stop exactly where they were on the floor. Dad would walk on the floor and correct a positioning mistake by one of the players. I froze in my stance with one hand in V's face and the other hand out. Dad started to coach the team as he made positioning corrections, and I tuned out. I knew what he was saying and I guess I was a little bored. I started to move my index finger in a circle around V's eye. Then I pulled a three stooges move and poked him in the eye. V was trying not to laugh. He faked like he was about to throw the ball at my groin. I flinched of course. All this happened while Dad had his back to us, but I swear it was like he had eyes in the back of his head. He turned around and slowly walked toward us with his eyebrows pointed downward to the bridge of his nose.

As he got closer, he said in a low voice, "I am about this close to burying my fist right in your face."

Bring it on, old man, is what I wanted to say, but I just glared at him.

"You wanna be a clown?" he said. He grabbed the ball from V and gave me a pretty strong shove with it toward the lobby doors. "Get out!" he yelled, at the top of his voice. "And take your clown buddy with you."

"Fine, I'm done!" I shot back, and slammed the door as I walked out.

He didn't have to tell me twice. I was already stressed out beyond belief from my shooting slump. Basketball wasn't fun anymore, and now I was pissed beyond belief too. I was a 21-year-old man, and I knew he never said anything like that to anyone he ever coached. Just me. I walked out the lobby doors, got my gear out of my locker, and drove home. I didn't want to play anymore.

When I got home I ate some dinner and went to my room. I put the movie "Fight Club" on and did some school work. I was totally brooding. I heard Dad get home around 6:30, and didn't want to see him or talk to him. I was just going to quit the team and that was that. I was in my room with the lights off and the T.V. on around 7:00, when Dad peeked his head in the door. I pretended to be asleep. He closed the door and let me be.

The next morning, I woke up at 6:00 am and left for the library before daylight, so I wouldn't have to see

Dad at breakfast. I was so angry and stressed out that I didn't want to give him a chance to apologize or talk me into coming back.

My original plan was to not even show up for practice that day. After my last class I walked to the gym. I didn't even plan on going there, but McGilvary Gym pulled me in with its tractor beam. I walked into the locker room to get some of my stuff. There was a post-it in Dad's handwriting on my locker that said: *J.T. Come see me.*

His office was right next to the locker room. He was sitting at his desk when I walked in and sat on the couch. He looked at me and started to tear up.

"Josh, I'm sorry," he said, "I have no excuse."

I knew he did, though. He had not been himself since the diabetes had taken hold.

"It's okay," I said. "I was clowning around." For some reason, I could never stay mad when he apologized.

"No it's not. My reaction was totally unnecessary. You're a grown man. You don't deserve that," he said. "Also, I just want you to play stress free basketball. It kills me to see you like this."

"I don't know how to fix it," I said.

"Well for one, I don't need to make it worse for you like I did yesterday. I crossed a line that should never be crossed. That won't ever happen again," he said. "Let's make a deal."

"Okay?" I said.

"I will always treat you like the grown man you are, but you gotta stop putting so much pressure on yourself. Let go," he said.

"I'll try," I replied.

"Good. The best way to quit stressing about your game is to get outside yourself and focus on being a great teammate," he said. "So, I'll see you at practice?"

"I was never quitting. I was just mad."

"I know," he said.

I went back to practice and tried to get outside myself. I tried to focus on making my teammates better, but my shot still wouldn't go in. I was still frustrated. The last game of the semester we played The University of Alabama at Huntsville. During the game, I missed a free throw and glanced at our bench. Everyone except Dad was giving me a different pointer to try and help my shooting form. My head was full of clutter. I took a step toward the bench and told them all to shut up. I shot terrible and didn't play any better. We lost by 20. It was a low point. We would take an 8-4 record into the Christmas break.

After the game, I stepped onto the bus with every intention to sit in the back and torture myself again with critical analysis followed by self-pity. Dad was in the front seat. He grabbed my arm as I walked by and pulled me toward him.

"Remember, we all thought you might die last spring." He knew I had hit bottom. He knew I needed some perspective.

"You didn't die," he said with a smile. I didn't know what to say.

I walked back to my seat and sat alone. What happened to me? I was so grateful to just be alive and healthy no more than four months ago. I wanted to live a balanced life, but old habits are hard to break. In a moment of clarity, Dad's words rang in my head...

"Quit thinking about it, it's not helping."

He was so right. I didn't care anymore. A smile crept across my face. When you finally hit bottom you can finally let go of your fear, and letting go was true freedom. Freedom of the mind. I closed my eyes as the music pumped through my headphones. I thought to myself, *It is great to be alive.*

49

WE DIDN'T HAVE A game for 27 days, so Dad gave us three weeks off. He was tired and needed a break from the stress of the season to get his diabetes under control. He always felt that a college basketball season is too long anyway. He also felt like we would be better by tournament time if we were all fresh coming into second semester. The break could not have come at a better time for me too. I didn't even touch a ball during the three weeks.

Before Christmas, I visited Abbie in D.C. for a week. We were starting to get serious. I met her parents and her brothers and absolutely loved her family. Fortunately for me, the feeling was mutual. Being around them was refreshing. As I spent more time with Abbie, I realized I was falling in love. This was new. She could floor me with a glance, and when I was around her my problems disappeared. I was a better person when I was with her. She opened up a door in my life that I never knew was there. Real, romantic love.

When I got back from D.C., I was enjoying living my life and being away from basketball. It was nice to be stress free and live a little. I would never go back to the way I used to be. Basketball was for a gym. Life was for living.

When it was time to get back in the gym for practice, I was ready and committed to my new mindset. I couldn't have cared less whether my shot went in. I played the game with passion and to the best of my ability. Every second on the court was mine to enjoy, and I planned to never waste another one of these precious seconds being lost in my own head again.

Our first game back we played Piedmont College from north Georgia. We were fresh, hungry, and played well. We had an 8-point lead with 2 minutes remaining when Piedmont began to foul. I went 6-6 from the line down the stretch to seal the victory, finished with 23 points, and was 11-11 from the line for the game. When Dad took me out in the final seconds, Jody said, "Welcome back, Josh," as I passed him. It was nice to be back.

We won 10 of our next 11 games. Our team was clicking, and Aaron Young and I were shooting the ball as well as we ever had. In a home win over Bryan College, I had a nasty collision when I went after a ball that was bouncing toward the sideline. When I went to scoop it up, I collided with one of their post players. At the same time, one of their guards dove for the ball and missed. His shoulder struck a hard blow to the outside of my lower right leg. The pain was intense, but I finished the game. A week passed, and the pain didn't go away. There was also a nasty bruise. Dad and the trainer made me go to the doctor to get x-rays. I didn't want to go because I felt like I could play through the pain. The x-rays showed that I had cracked my fibula. I feared the worst. I was sure the doc would shut me down for a while, but he said I could play as long as I could stand the pain. I would just have to wait until the off-season to let it completely heal. I was having way too much fun to let a little stress fracture stop me. What a relief!

In February, I asked Abbie to marry me. I knew we were young, but I just couldn't fathom my life without her. Somehow, I just knew. Not only was I madly in love with her, I liked her even more. She said, "Yes."

Abbie moved back home and started working at her old job at a bank to try to save some money so we could get married next summer. The long distance relationship was not easy, but we were going to make it work no matter what. People told us we were crazy because we were so young. Yes... we were crazy, but we didn't care.

Our final regular season game was at Pensacola

Christian College. Brad Green took the trip down with one of his high school buddies, Travis Broyles. Since Brad had moved back to Chattanooga, he sat on the front row across from the benches every home game and was my own personal trash talker. It felt nice to be on the other side of the heckling. He was hilarious. I thoroughly enjoyed giving him a lot of ammo to fire with his own cannon of verbal assaults.

Pensacola is an Independent Fundamental Baptist college with the strictest of rules put on their student body. I thought T.T.U. had a lot of rules. We were a party school compared to these poor souls. It was like a cult. Everyone looked the same, with the male students all having the same short comb over haircut and the girls all wearing long skirts. When you stepped foot on campus it was like you had just entered a foreign country. But boy did these people love 'em some basketball. We were a Baptist school as well, so I think they thought we were rivals, but we laid the smack down on them every time. We arrived at the arena two hours early, and there were already students standing in the ticket line. Maybe they just didn't have much else to do because they were pretty much on lock down all the time. Or maybe, just maybe, they thought this was their year to beat us.

This was their best team since I had been playing, and we would be in for a dog fight. The arena was packed. It was like an ocean of white polo shirts and parted comb overs. They had one group of students standing on the sideline across from the benches. At times during the game, these guys were literally on the court. And guess who stood right in the middle of this front line of P.C.C. clones. Brad and Travis. Brad had on a beanie, and Travis had hair down to his shoulders. It looked like they took a wrong turn somewhere on the way to a Kid Rock concert. They were about to take their trash talk game to a whole new level. They only needed us to give them some ammo. That night, I gave them a whole arsenal.

When the game started, the place was rocking as always, and it was like I went to another place. I dropped three after three. With each one, Brad and Travis celebrated in a more and more outlandish fashion. They partied up and down the sideline, surrounded by dejected clones. I was so hot that you could hear their crowd groan every time I looked at the rim. The game was close, but we would never trail. We won 78-72. I dropped a 40 spot on 9-12 from 3. It was a rush.

We would play Pensacola again in the first round of the South Region tournament. This time, Aaron would set it off. He knocked down 7 threes and dropped 33. We won 96-76. We took care of North Greenville University in the semifinals 63-53. It would be us and

NCAA Division 1 Gardner Webb in the championship game again. The Bulldogs got off to a quick start, shooting over 60%, and had a 24-point lead in the first half. We clawed our way back and got within striking distance with 4 minutes to play, cutting the lead to 8, but couldn't quite get over the hump. They were too deep and too talented. Our season would end with a 75-62 loss.

Aaron and I were named to the All-Region team, and I was named second team NCCAA All-American. I shot over 45% from 3 and 90% from the line after I quit worrying about my shooting. Dad knew it all along. He raised me to be a player, not a shooter. I grew up shooting stress free, but after the debacle from the charity stripe at Lee, it just snowballed and I had lost my way. Dad knew what I needed and he had the perfect words for me. It was only a few words, but they held the power of liberation that perspective and a clear mind bring. I learned that you CAN want it TOO much. My obsession was over. I would keep balance in my life and never forget the real reason why I played—because I loved to play the game.

Having fun again

50

THE SUMMER OF 2002 would be my final off-season as a player. I was at the top of my game, but I still wanted to add something to my game during the summer. This summer would be different. My addition would not be in the strength or skills department. It would be mental. I would make myself take a step away from the game. The concept of living a balanced life changed me, but it didn't change my passion for basketball. That would never go away. It changed the person I was. This time next year, I would no longer be a college basketball player. I wasn't sure what the future had in store for me, but I was going to enjoy everything life had to offer, every single day.

I moved out of the house and rented a 1-bedroom apartment, and was ready to start my own family with Abbie. Abbie and I got married on August 16, 2002, and Dad was my best man. It was the best day of my life. I married my best friend with the man who showed me how to be a man by my side. Abbie and I went on our honeymoon during the first week of school, and I was in no hurry to get back.

When I finally showed up on campus, I could see that Dad did some serious recruiting over the summer. I knew he was in on some good freshman, but I had been gone for a month, so I didn't know how the recruiting season ended up. This group was something special. Adam Asberry was a 6'2" shooting guard who played for the Upperman Bees in high school. He was a freshman when they ended my high school career and could really fill it up. 6'4" guard Javier Sanchez was an exchange student from Spain that was an incredible talent who could score in many different ways. Somehow Dad got 6'6" point forward Josh Jones from Bradley Central High School, which is practically next door to Lee University. Josh was the best passer I ever played with.

In addition to these guys, you wouldn't believe who transferred in, our old friend Keith Galloway. Keith was playing at U. T. Chattanooga but decided to come to T.T.U. and play with us for his final year of eligibility. Caleb Marcum was also playing baseball at T.T.U. He saw that we were going to be good and jumped on the bandwagon as well. Caleb was one of the best pitchers on our baseball team, and was such a ridiculous athlete that he could just decide to play basketball out of nowhere and earn minutes on the best team Temple had in over a decade. In fact, by the time the season started, he was starting at guard and was our lock down defender.

With a strong core of seniors (Craig Price, Andre Dubois, Nathan Ranew, and I), a host of talented freshman, and the addition of Caleb and Keith, expectations were high for my senior season. It would be a going out party of sorts, and it turned out to be a pretty good party.

I played some pick up ball on the day after me and Abbie returned from our honeymoon, and I was rusty. My timing was way off because I hadn't played in over a month. I had never taken that much time off in my life, but basketball was like riding a bike. It wouldn't take long to get back into game shape.

We had six home games to open the season and won all six. One of which was against Lee. Lee had their best team in the Rick Hughes era. They were even more talented than the 2000-2001 Flames. We spread the floor with shooters. Every player Dad put in the game was a good 3-point shooter. This opened up many opportunities for me to get into the paint, because the defense was so spread out. If they helped, which they usually did, I would find my teammates for open shots. And my teammates would make them pay. Coach Hughes tried to guard me with his point guard coalition, and as a result, Chuckie and Frank both fouled out in the game. I ended up with 22 points on 8 shot attempts and went 11-11 from the free throw line. We had beaten Lee 81-77.

Bringing it up vs. Chuckie Campbell

Next, we took our show to the road and played NCAA Division 2 opponent Kennesaw State. Kennesaw ran a player at me every time I crossed half court. That game was one of the few games all season that we didn't shoot the ball well. They kicked our butts 78-65. Kennesaw had everybody from this team back the next year and won the NCAA Division 2 national championship. It was safe to say they were pretty good.

But we weren't down for long. We ran off seven straight to take a 13-1 record into the Christmas break. It was the second best start in school history. Dad gave us another long break to refresh.

After the break, we played in a classic at Georgia Southwestern University. Our first game was on January 3rd, and we didn't have to be back at practice until the 1st. Dad always thought long-term. I think he hoped deep down we would lose a game or two right after Christmas. He knew every team needs a good soul cleansing before the tournament run.

That is exactly what happened. We weren't satisfied by any means, but we were rusty because we didn't have much time to practice before the Holiday Classic. Have you ever heard the term 'First Day Hots?' It is when you take some time out of the gym, then come back and make everything you put up. It seemed that always happened to me after a break. My mind was refreshed. I had fresh legs and was virtually unstoppable against Georgia Southwestern, making 9 threes on 13 attempts, on my way to a 35-point performance. But we lost 88-84.

The next day against Brewton Parker, it was more of the same. I went 8-14 from three and had 30. We lost that game as well. For a minute on the way home, I was pissed, but I remembered what Dad had told me years earlier when I was a senior in high school...

"Nobody plays defense as well when they are not involved in the offense."

"Get your teammates more involved."

"There is no need for heroics on a good team."

"Trust your teammates."

Because I had been coached so well growing up, I was at the point now where I could coach myself. That angry moment was gone before our bus got on the interstate. With Dad's help, I had learned the most valuable lesson of my life the semester before. There is no greater misery than living a life consumed with your own story. You miss out on life when you are stuck inside yourself. He taught me this over and over growing up, but I would forget at times. I guess I had to learn this truth on my own, but now, I finally got it. I could think about the game with total objectivity now because my life was balanced and my head was clear, and I knew I had to do a better job of making my teammates better.

I talked to Craig for a while in the hotel that night. As the leaders of this team, we would take total responsibility for the loss when we got back to practice. We would pour our knowledge and experience into the freshman and were committed to setting them up for success. When one of them would check into the game, we would get them an easy shot early to get them into the flow.

The next game we played at Tennessee Wesleyan, and they decided they were not going to let me beat them. They double teamed me all night, but that was just fine with me. I knew my teammates would make them pay. Craig carried the scoring load with 17 that night and I had 14 assists.

Everyone we played had Caleb pegged as the guy you could give big help off of, because he didn't shoot much. This plan didn't work out so well because he made a 3-pointer for our first bucket of the game in 10 games that year. They would start off giving big help off of him, and without hesitating, he would drain one right off the bat. They would immediately be forced to rethink their strategy. He didn't shoot much because he didn't have to. His role on this team was to put the other team's best scorer on lock-down. He was the ulti-mate team guy who just loved playing ball and checked his ego at the door every time he laced 'em up. He had a role and he attacked it. This was the best offensive team I'd ever played on. If our opponents focused on one or two guys, the rest of our guys would always make them question their decision.

We won 10 in a row, including another win ver-sus Lee at Paul Dana Walker Arena. Craig set Lee's game plan on fire by stepping out and knocking down four 3's on six attempts. It felt good to sweep Lee in our final season. What made it even sweeter was that Lee won the Southern States Athletic Conference and made it to the Elite Eight in the NAIA national tournament. We had beaten them when they were at their best. We took a 25-4 record into the NCCAA South region tournament and won it handily. Next on the slate was the National Tournament at the Frankfurt Civic Center in Frankfurt, Kentucky.

51

WE ENTERED THE EIGHT team national tournament as the top seed. As a team, we were shooting over 41% from 3 on the year, and I was having a dream season shooting the ball. I averaged 23 points and 7.8 assists per game. Both of which led the nation in their respective statistical categories. Craig, Javier, and Adam each averaged 10 points per game. Josh Jones was our second leading rebounder and assist man in his role off the bench. His basketball I.Q. was something special, and it was no coincidence that my scoring average went up by 7 points when I started playing with Josh. We were like peanut butter and jelly. He could get me the ball exactly where I wanted it at any time, as if we had been playing together for years. Keith and Andre brought some scoring punch off the bench as well, and Nathan Renew played the role of enforcer, setting some of the most vicious screens that our 1-4 high offense had ever seen. Playing with these guys reminded me of the chemistry of our good teams in high school. We just loved to win, and we loved each other, so everyone was willing to sacrifice for the team. Teams like this come around once a lifetime if you are lucky. This was the third one I had played on, and they were all coached by Dad. I felt like the luckiest player on the planet.

The day before we left for the tournament I decided to stay after practice for a few minutes to get up some shots. Dad came over and rebounded for me. He didn't say a word. I didn't say a word. I shot, and he rebounded and passed to me. I couldn't help but notice he had a smile on his face the whole time.

"What are you smiling about?" I said.

"I'm just enjoying this, my man," he replied. "You know, I never thought this day would come, but this is probably going to be the last time I get to do this."

What started out to be just getting up a few shots at the end of practice, ended up being more than an hour of shooting, rebounding and passing. Neither of us wanted to leave. Neither of us said another word. We just enjoyed the moment together.

After we were done I went to the locker room to

pack my gear. As I went out to my car to head home, Dad was getting in his car at the same time.

"Dad," I said, as he was opening his car door.

"Yeah?" he answered.

"I wanna win so bad," I confessed.

"I know, Josh. I want it for you."

"I'm not going to be worried about shooting well. You know I'm past all that, but what if it just doesn't fall," I said.

"You'll still play your guts out like you always do, and I'm going to have the best time I've ever had coaching this game... because I only get three more games to coach you."

I was a 22-year-old married man. When he said stuff like this, my heart still felt like it would swell to five times its original size.

"I just want you to do one thing. If not for yourself, then for me. Promise me," Dad said.

"Anything, Dad."

"Just go out there and enjoy it. All the work you've done, all the adversity you've faced, all we've been through together has gotten us here. There's nothing left to do to prepare. You've already done it. Now just go out there and enjoy it. You have 120 minutes left to play college basketball. Play the game like you have all year long. Like the little kid who just loves to compete

307

and seizes the moment. I know I've told you this over and over again, but you know it to be true. Watching you play is one of my favorite things in the world."

He started to tear up, "I'm gonna miss it so much."

"Thanks, Dad. I love you."

"I love you too, Josh. You're gonna play great."

"WE are gonna play great," I said, as we got in our cars and drove away.

52

MUCH LIKE OUR HIGH school teams at Temple, we didn't look like much. Craig was not used to people laughing at our lack of size like me and Caleb. We had been there, done that. During a banquet held in the Civic Center the night before the tournament, our guys walked in, and a handful of players from Oklahoma Wesleyan started whispering and laughing at our size. You would think that college players would know better than to judge a book by its cover. I don't think these guys were academic All-Americans though. It doesn't matter what level of college basketball you are playing on, if a team is 27-4, it's probably not in your best interest to piss them off. Especially if they look like a group of Mormon missionaries.

I came in a little late because I rode up with Abbie, and we ran into some traffic. When I walked in, the room was pretty quiet. They had already begun the program when I spotted our tables next to Oklahoma Wesleyan. As I walked to my seat, this mouthy guy from Oklahoma Wesleyan said to his teammates at his table, "That's the guy? Naaawwww man." And they all started laughing. This dude was obnoxious, talking out loud so our entire team could hear him. Looking back, I'm not really sure what he was trying to accomplish. Was he trying to intimidate us or was he just a punk? I smiled at them as I walked by, thinking to myself, *Yes, this is the guy. You better pray to the basketball gods that you don't see us in the semifinals.* I actually liked the attention. It meant I must have been doing something right for them to be already talking about me. Craig was pissed. I had never seen him this angry.

"I'll be rooting for them hard tomorrow. I want to play them so bad. And I'll make sure you drop forty on that guy," he said.

I laughed, "It's all good, my man. I'm used to this. You're not?"

"No. I'm not," he said, serious as a heart attack.

Caleb busted up in laughter. "Mouthy guy's like that never hold up their end of the bargain," he said.

He was right. The next day Oklahoma Wesleyan got trashed by Bethel College from Indiana.

We would open up against the talented 8 seed Crichton College from Memphis, Tennessee. Crichton was a group of talented D1 and JUCO transfers from Memphis. They were led by prolific scorer Mario Cain. I scored 30 points and dished out 10 assists as we cruised to a 94-77 win. We all joked about how Caleb held Mario to 27 points, but he really did a great job on him. Mario had 45 on a tournament record 10 threes in the consolation bracket game against Oklahoma Wesleyan the next day. Craig got a kick out of that.

We played the Pilots of Bethel College in the semifinals the next afternoon. It was a nip and tuck affair that featured six lead changes and three ties in the first half. I started hot, but picked up my second foul with 8 minutes left in the half. Bethel hit a 3 at the horn to give them a 5-point advantage at halftime.

We stormed out of the halftime locker room and built a 9-point lead with 12 minutes remaining, thanks to dominating post play by Craig. He was unstoppable on the block during this stretch, scoring over either shoulder at will against much bigger defenders. Bethel slowly chipped at our lead and found themselves down by 4 points with the ball and 29 seconds remaining. They banked in an off-balance 3-point shot with 16 seconds to cut it to 1. The Pilots called timeout to set their press.

After the timeout, Craig inbounded the ball and

we moved it across the floor rarely taking a dribble. Our spacing was perfect and it looked like a game of keep away on the Highland Park outdoor courts. Every time they got close enough to one of us to foul, the ball was already gone. We ran out the clock and held on for an 82-81 win. We would move on to the national championship game. I had 29 points and 9 assists, but Craig was the big difference maker in this game. He dominated them inside the entire game, posting 22 points and 8 rebounds.

If we were to win a national championship, we would have to go through the Lancers of Grace College. They were led by NCCAA player of the year Matt Abernathy. Craig was pissed about this too. He thought I should have been named player of the year. Come to think of it, Craig was pretty pissed the whole tournament. I guess it was a good thing, because Craig was great when he played angry.

Craig playing angry

53

THE LOCKER ROOM WAS quiet. The mood was serious. In less than 30 minutes we would be playing for a national championship. I sat on a bench between Caleb and Keith. I started to pull out the contents of my bag. I pulled my trademark high red socks over my taped ankles, then laced up my Team Edition Nike Shox. I looked in my bag. Only one thing left. My white Temple #3 jersey. I held it in my hands. This would be the last time I would put it on, and the last game I ever played.

As I sat there deep in thought, Dad walked in. He was a master in the art of pre-game motivation, and all eyes were locked on him as he began his speech.

"I want you to close your eyes."

"Think of the moments in your basketball

journey that got you to this point. Sitting in this room. Getting ready to play for a national championship."

"I want you to remember why you started playing in the first place."

"See yourself as a little kid. A little kid playing the game for the sheer joy of playing."

"See yourself in the gym. Putting up shots with no one around."

"See yourself making plays and celebrating the greatest moments of your career."

"Then visualize what you are about to do. See yourself playing the game of your life in the national championship."

"See yourself cutting down the nets with your brothers."

"Don't move, just keep your eyes closed and take your journey."

A familiar piano tune began to play. Dave Barrett's *One Shining Moment* would be the soundtrack to our journey through visualization. As the song played, I could see the moments just as if they were happening right then...

Battling on the outdoor courts of Highland Park...

Shirtless, soaked in sweat, putting up a shot in the Vance Gym...

A bear hug from Higgs after winning the district championship...

The opening tip of the state championship game...

Breaking down in the locker room after the ending of my high school career...

Draining a 3 and seeing Brad run the entire sideline taunting thousands of fans...

Dishing it off to Craig for a game sealing 3 pointer at Paul Dana Walker Arena...

Holding up the Region Championship banner with my boys...

As the final notes faded out, I could see myself cutting down the nets.

I opened my eyes.

Dad was standing in front of us. "This is your moment. Go get it."

54

GRACE LED BY FOUR early until Craig started to show Abernathy who was boss. He scored 8 points in the paint in the first 8 minutes of the game. That opened things up for me as I drained three 3's later in the half and we built a 7-point lead. Grace scored 6 straight to cut our lead to 1 right before half, but I responded by hitting a runner at the buzzer to give us a 3-point advantage at the break.

They started to double Craig inside in the second half. This opened the flood gates for our long range bombs. We hit eight 3's in the second half, including three by senior Andre Dubois in a 65 second stretch that pushed our lead up to 21 points. With 1:30 remaining, the horn sounded. I looked at the scoreboard. We were up big. I looked at the scorer's table. I was coming out. I didn't want to leave the floor. This was it. It was over. Tear's filled my eyes. As I walked toward the bench, I looked up into the stands and saw my wife. She looked so happy for me. I walked toward Dad who was standing on the sideline with his arms wide open. He had a smile on his face with a tear streaming down his cheek. I walked to him, and we embraced.

"We did it, Josh," he said.

All I could say was two words, "Thank you." I don't even know if he heard me, because my face was buried in his shoulder. I was trying hard not to break down right there in front of everyone.

The final horn sounded. Our team stormed the floor and a dog pile ensued. We cut down the nets and took pictures with our national championship banner. I hugged my wife. I hugged her family. I hugged my family. I hugged everyone. Then I took the long walk down the tunnel to the locker room, where the celebration continued. I thanked every one of my teammates who made this year special.

As I shared moments with my friends, a somber spirit began to take over me. I wanted to be happy. Happy for Dad. Happy for my teammates. Happy for myself. But I was becoming overcome with sadness. As the celebrating continued, I walked into the showers. I couldn't bring myself to take off the jersey. I couldn't believe it was over. I was no longer a player. That part of me died right there. I crouched facing a corner and it all came out. I wept. I grieved for the player inside who had died. As I began to reflect on my career, the tears of sadness began to turn into tears of gratitude. I closed my eyes and could see more snippets of my basketball journey:

The little boy making the shot then falling to the floor at halftime...

Opening my letter from Dad after 5th grade camp...

Sitting in the doctor's office with Dad getting bad news...

Falling to my knees on the floor and looking at Dad after our loss in the state championship...

Looking at Dad then draining a deep kill shot in the District Championship...

Dad pulling me aside on the bus to remind me to love life...

Winning a national championship.

Dad was there for everything. Dad taught me more through basketball than I learned in all my college classes combined. There was no one that had more fun playing this game than I did, and it was because of him. He made it fun. He let it be fun. He wasn't always perfect, and neither was I, but that is real life. It was not a fairy tale, but a journey of passion, resiliency, heart, discovery, and a father's love.

I was overwhelmed with gratitude for every moment on my journey...

For everything Dad did...

For him having the courage to not care about what anyone else thought...

For him being hard on me to hold me to the standard of excellence I had set for myself...

For him teaching me how to be a man...

For him showing me the importance of living a balanced life...

For him having the confidence in me to let me be the man I wanted to be...

For believing in me.

I walked out of the shower with my jersey still on. Dad was the only one left. I walked up to him with my eyes swollen. We didn't say a word. We embraced and cried. We walked out together, but before he opened the door he looked directly into my eyes and said it one more time...

"Josh, I'm so proud of you."

About the Author

Josh is the son of Kevin Templeton, one of the most well respected coaches in the southeast. Always around basketball growing up, he developed a deep passion for the game at a very early age.

He had a blessed basketball career despite being 5'9' 150 pounds. His high school career included an opportunity to play in a TSSAA state championship game as well as being nominated for Mr. Basketball in Tennessee. After high school, he played at Tennessee Temple University where he was a two-time All-American and scored over 2,000 points while TTU compiled 95 wins in 4 years. He holds the school record for single season 3-pointers made and career assists.

After graduation, Josh served as an assistant at his alma mater with his father for 4 years from 2003-2007. From 2007-2012, he assisted Tommy Brown at Lee University. During those 5 years, Lee saw an unprecedented run of success with a record of 130-36. He has been headlining Coach T basketball camps with his Dad for the last 15 years as well as serving as a director for Point Guard College for the last 3 years. He is currently running a player development program in Chattanooga called All In Hoops. He and Abbie, his wife of 14 years, have two daughters, Alivia (11), and Layla (4). You can find him on his blog where he shares his thoughts on basketball, parenting, the mental approach, and player development at CoachTHoops.com and on twitter @joshtempleton37